Doodle Coloring Book For Adults To Relax and Relieve Stress

This book belongs to:

_____

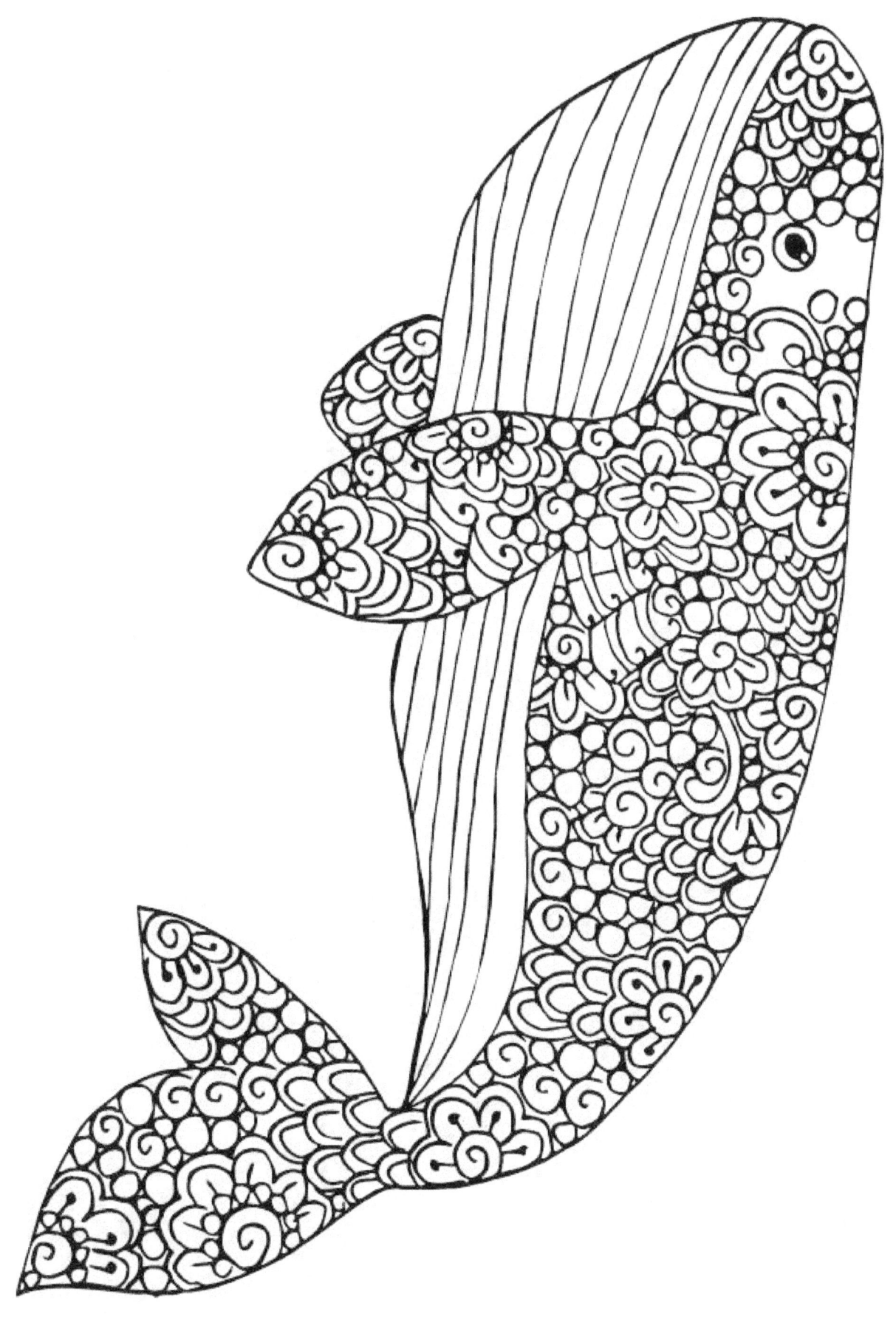

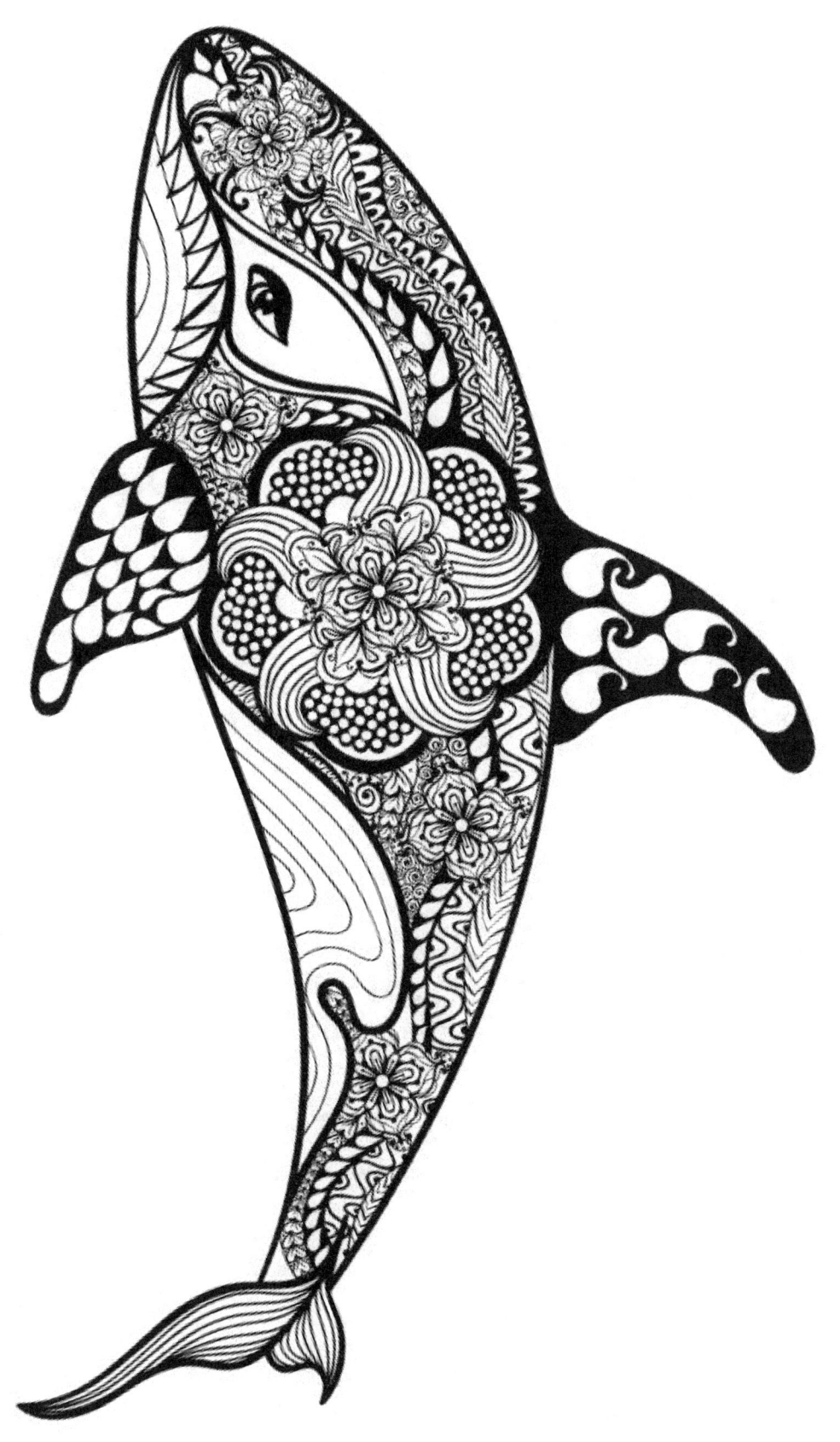

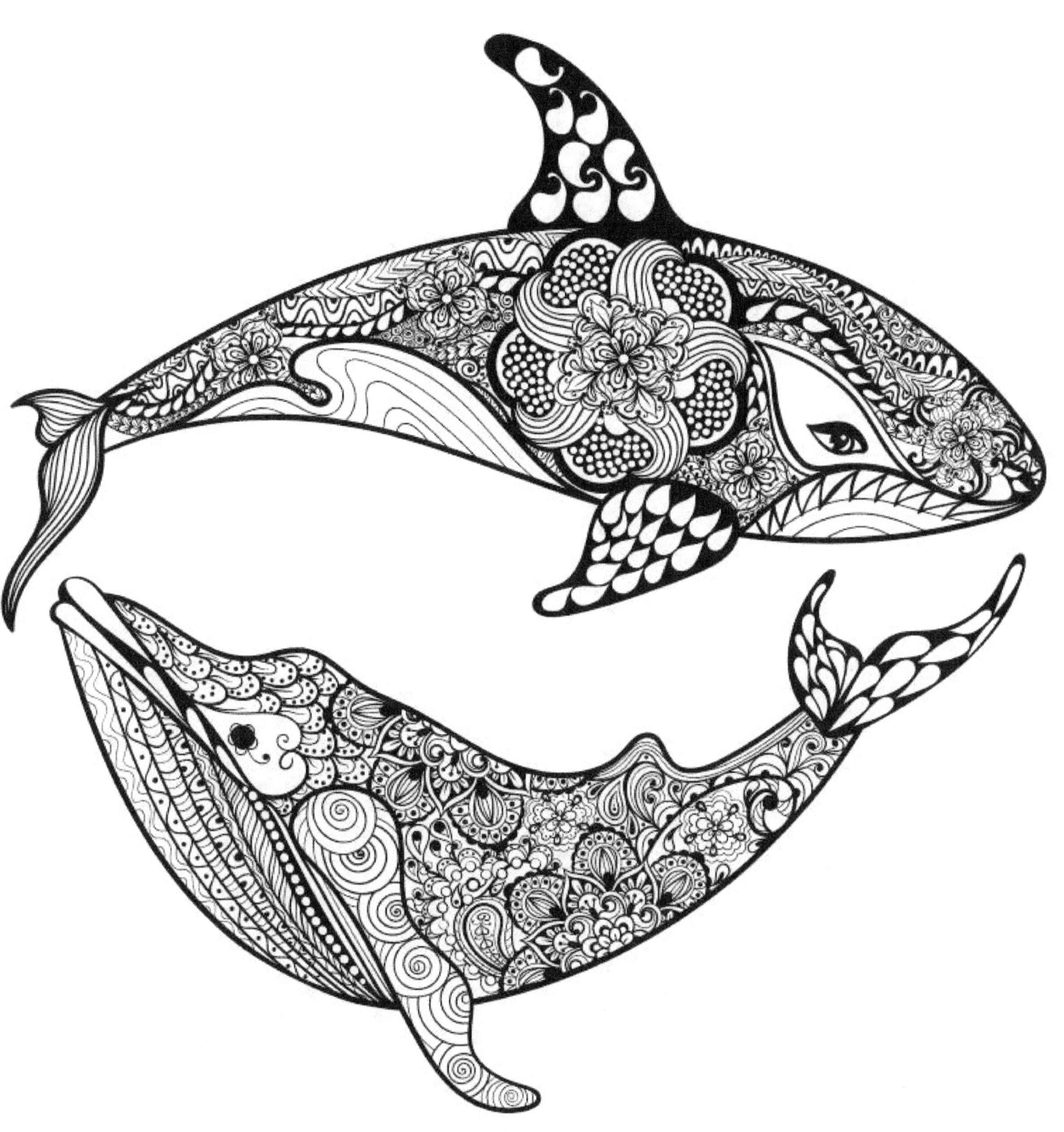

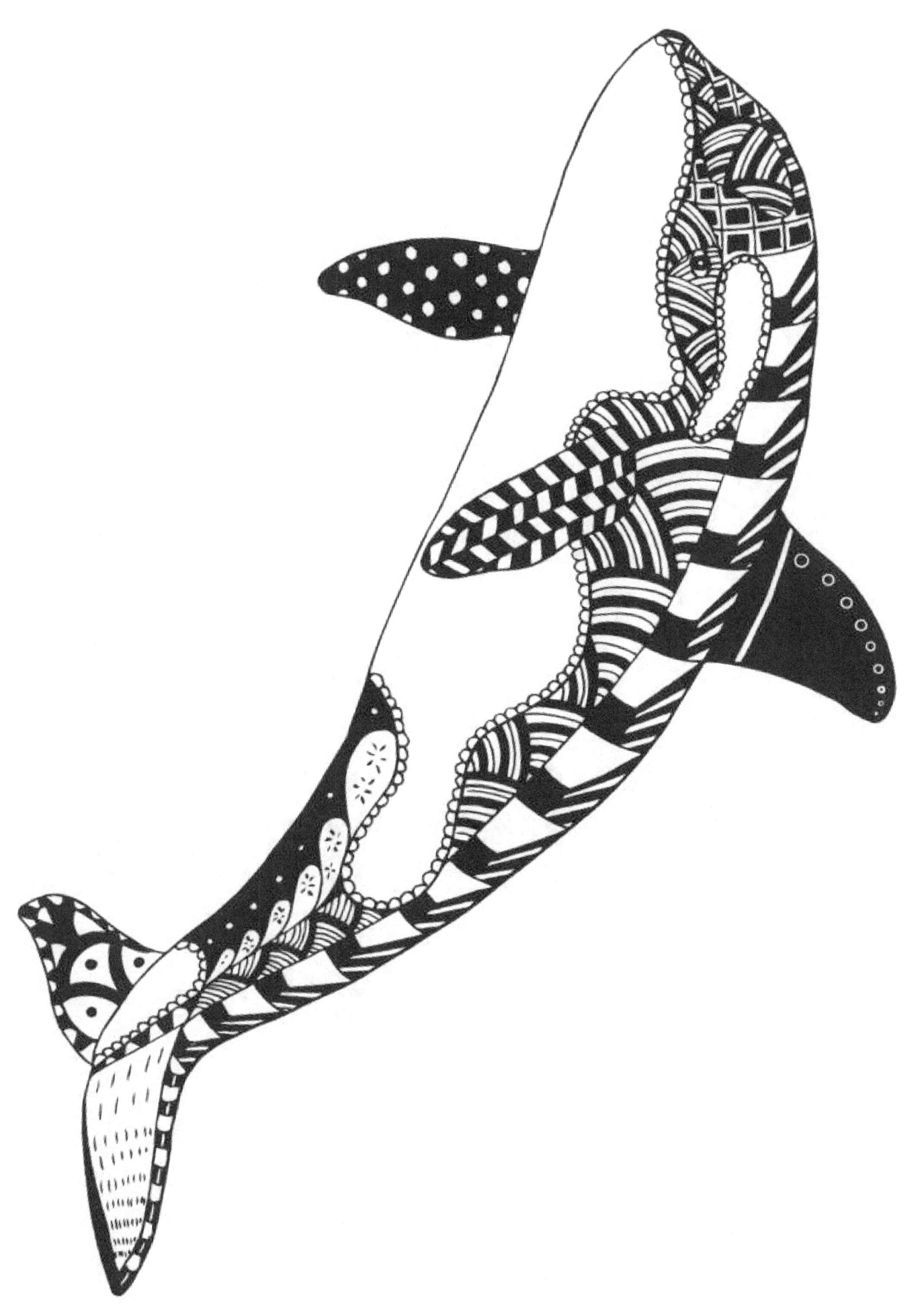

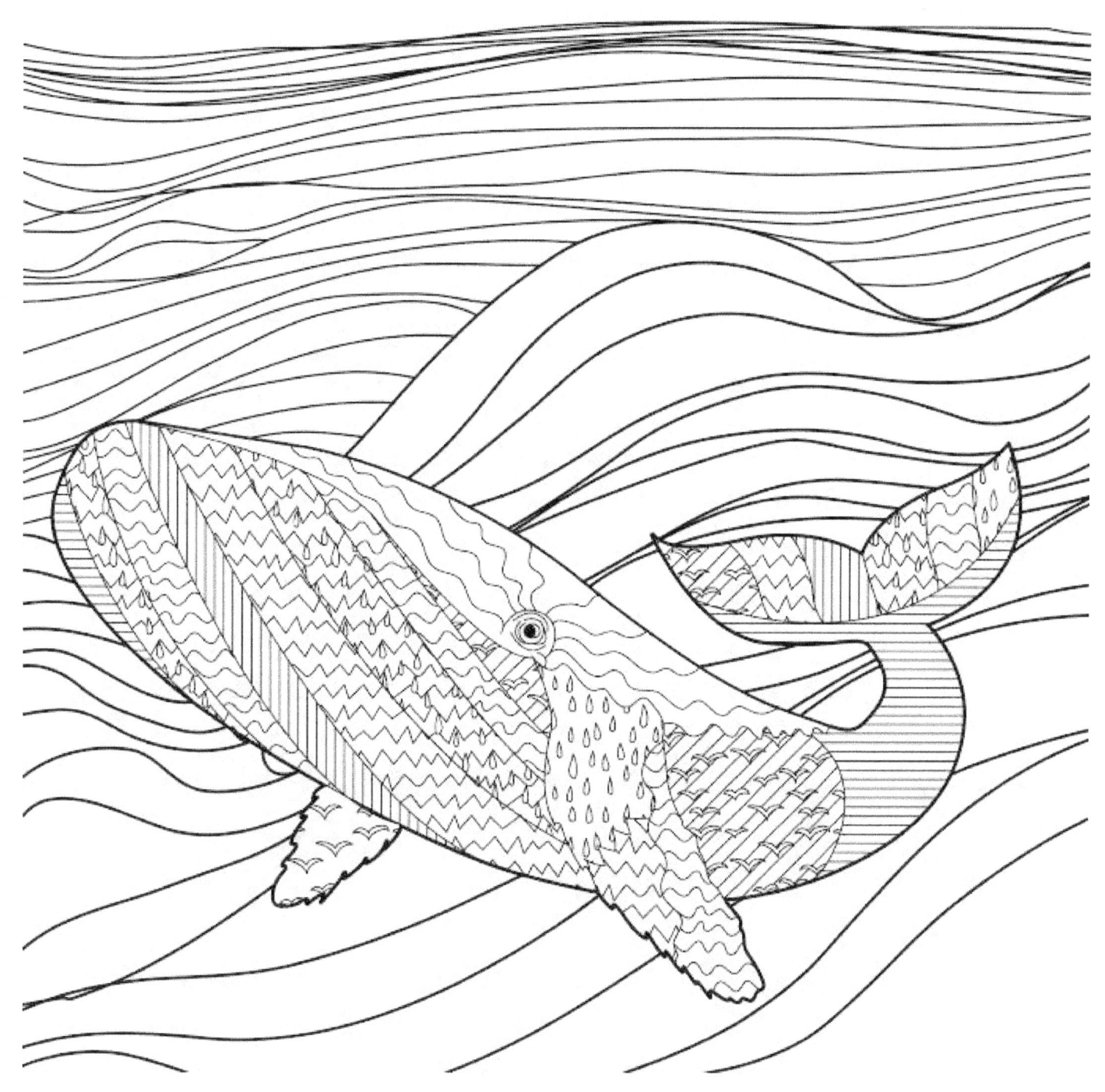

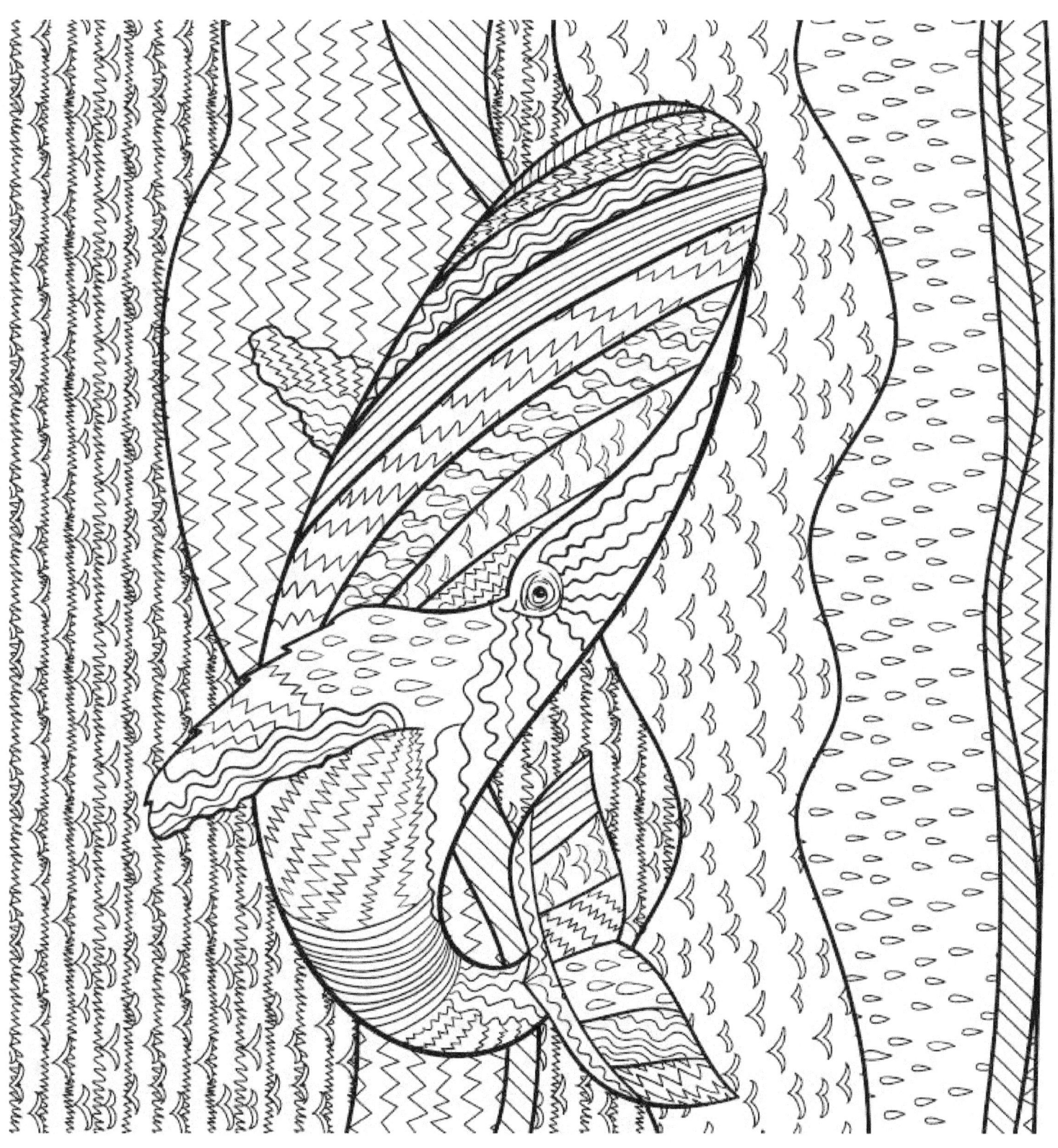

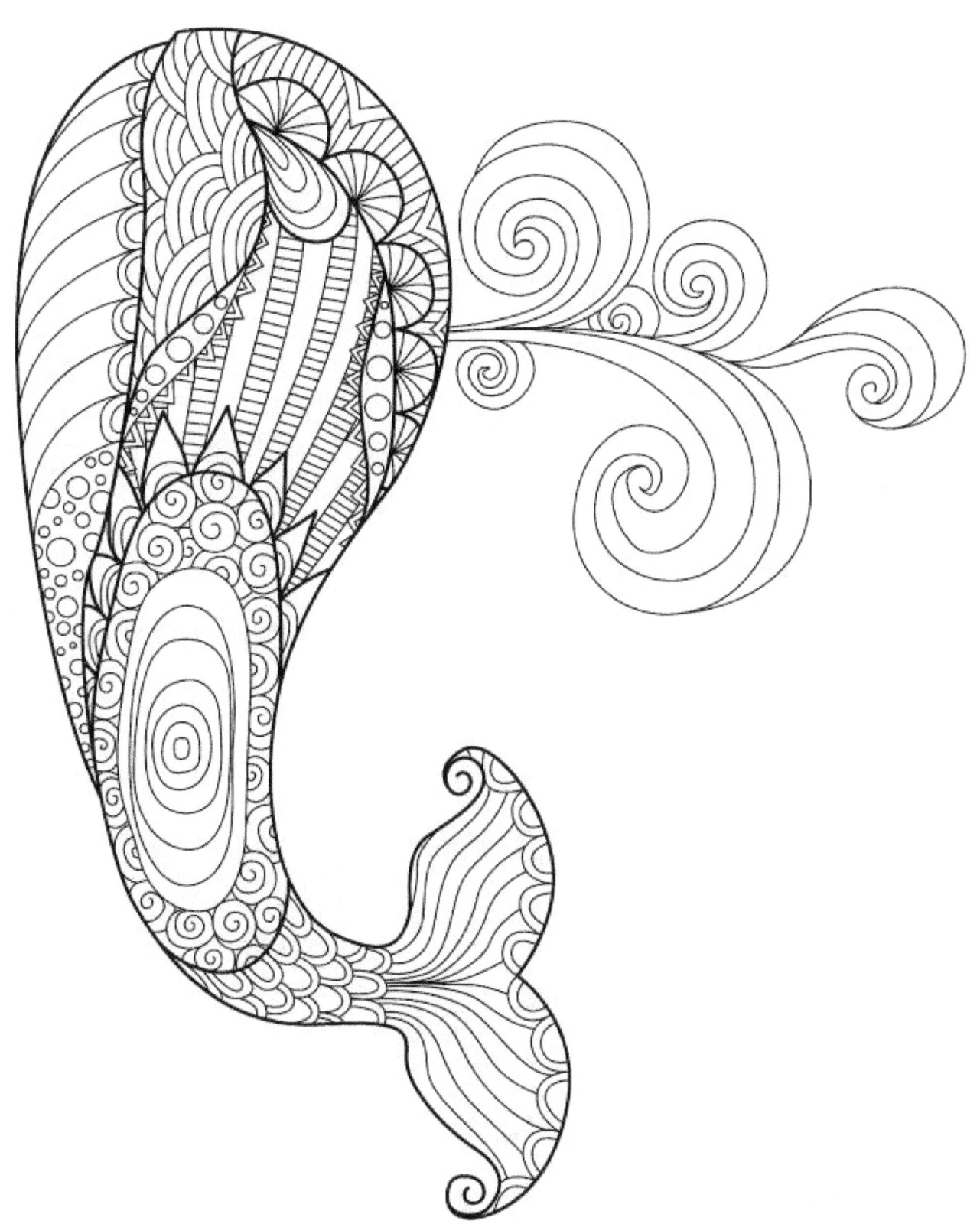

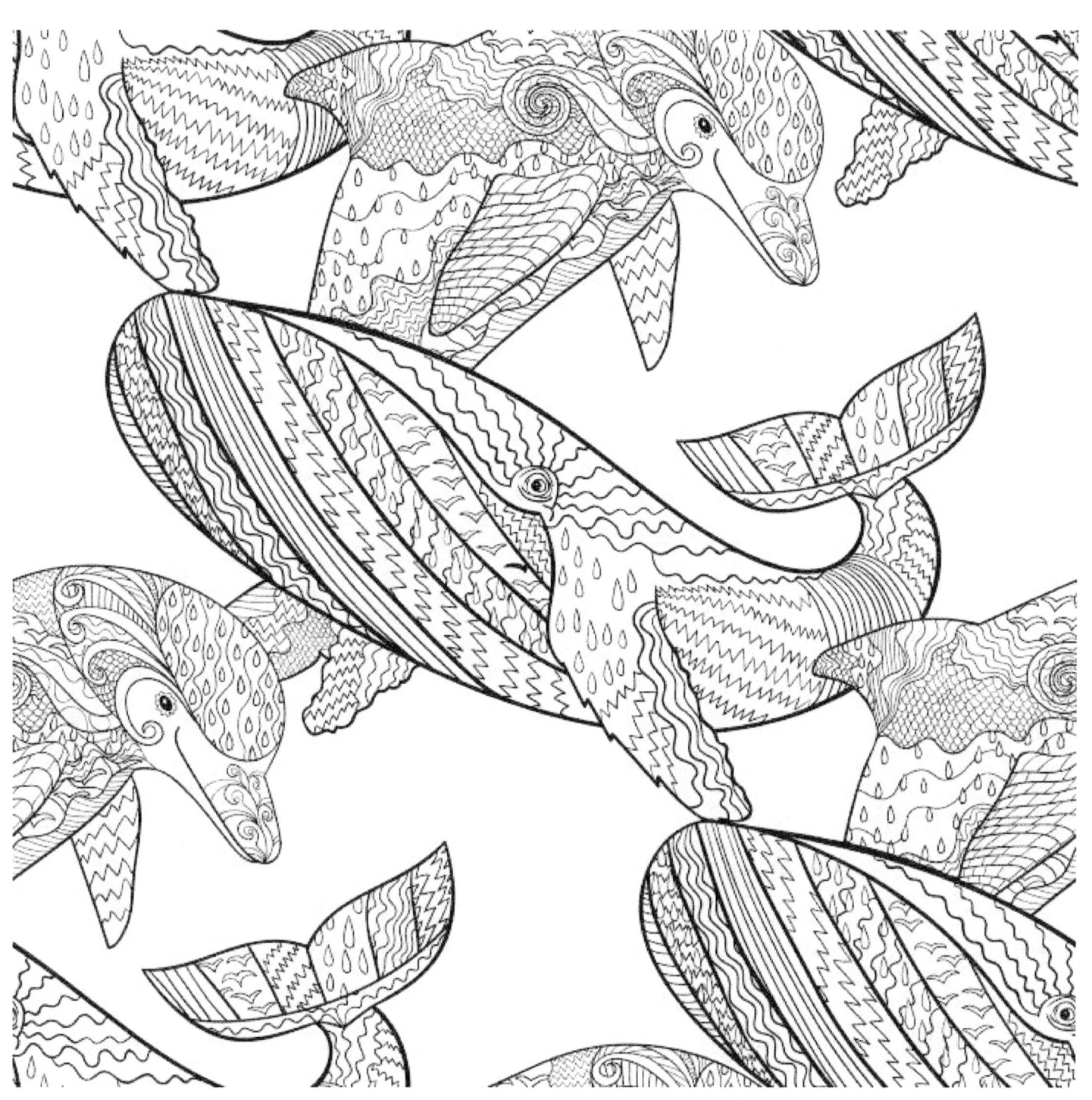

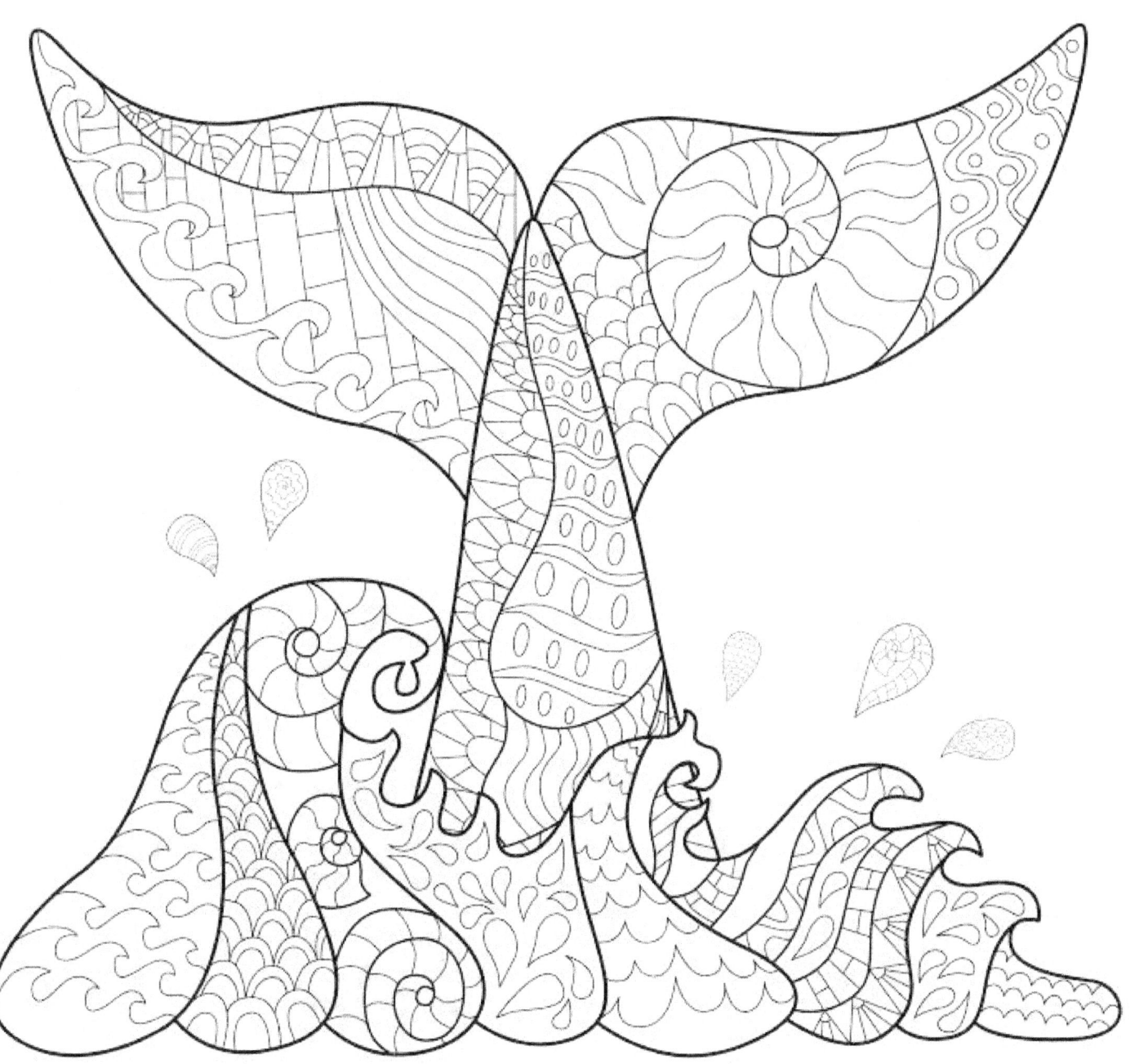

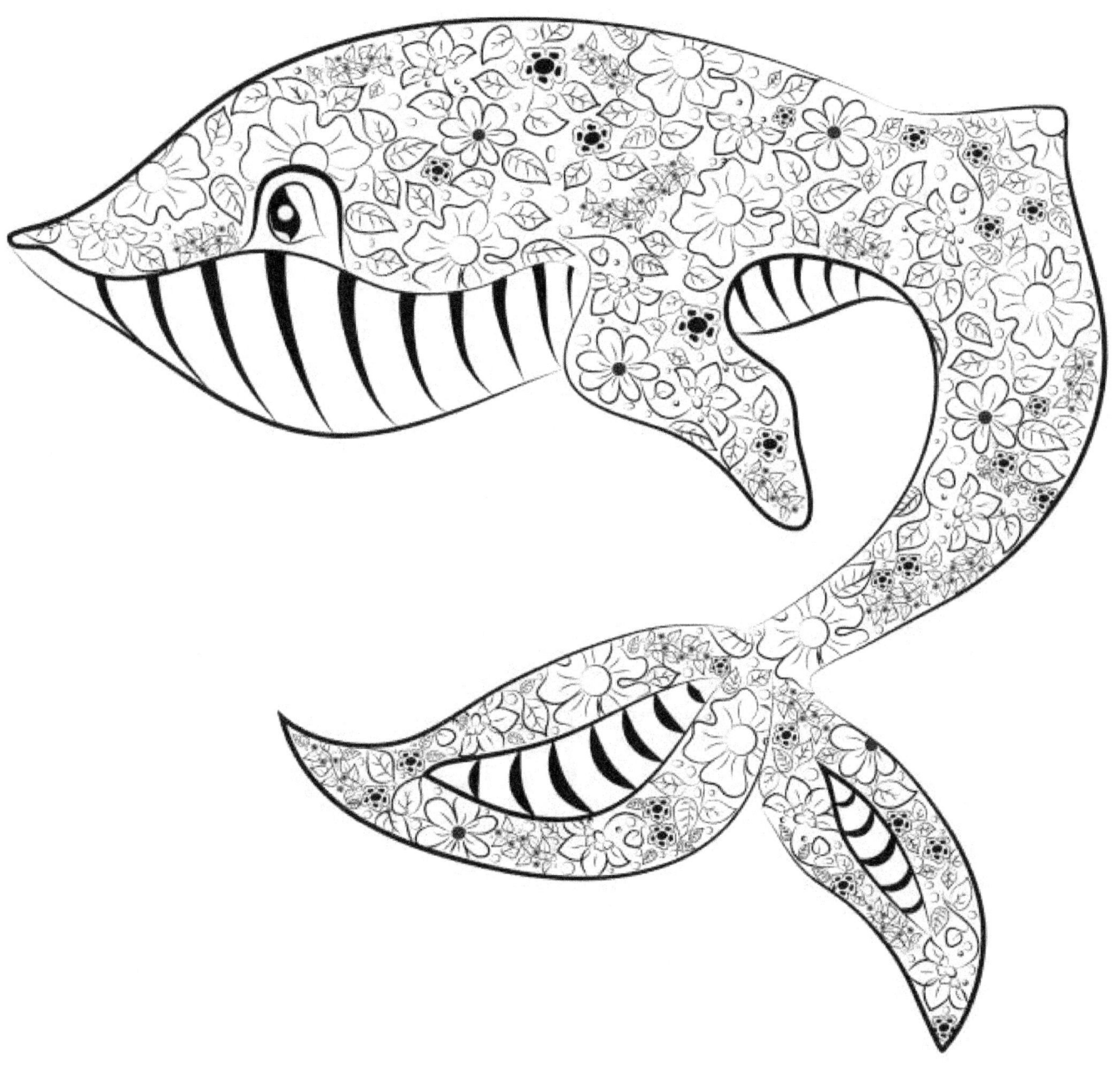

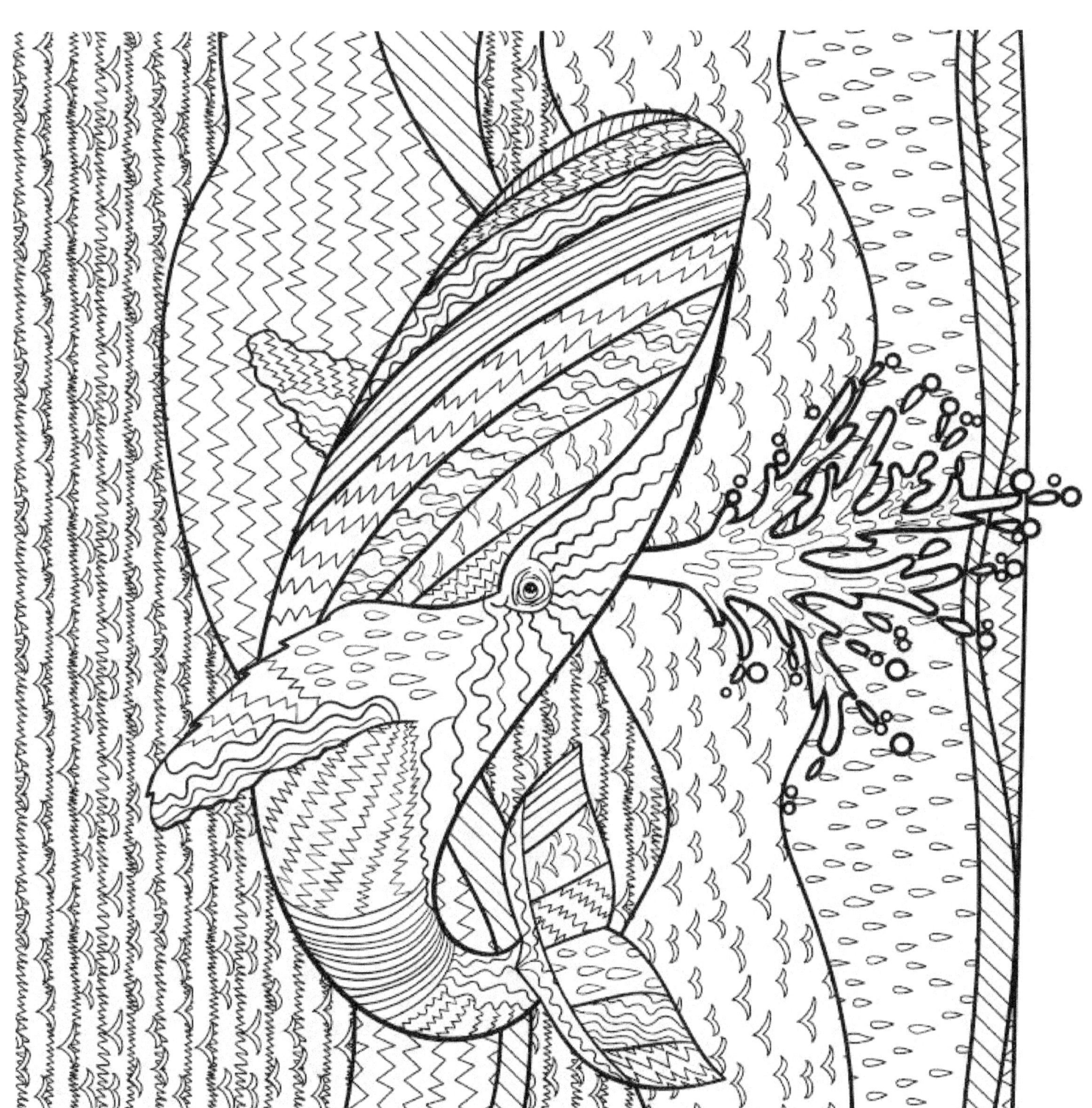

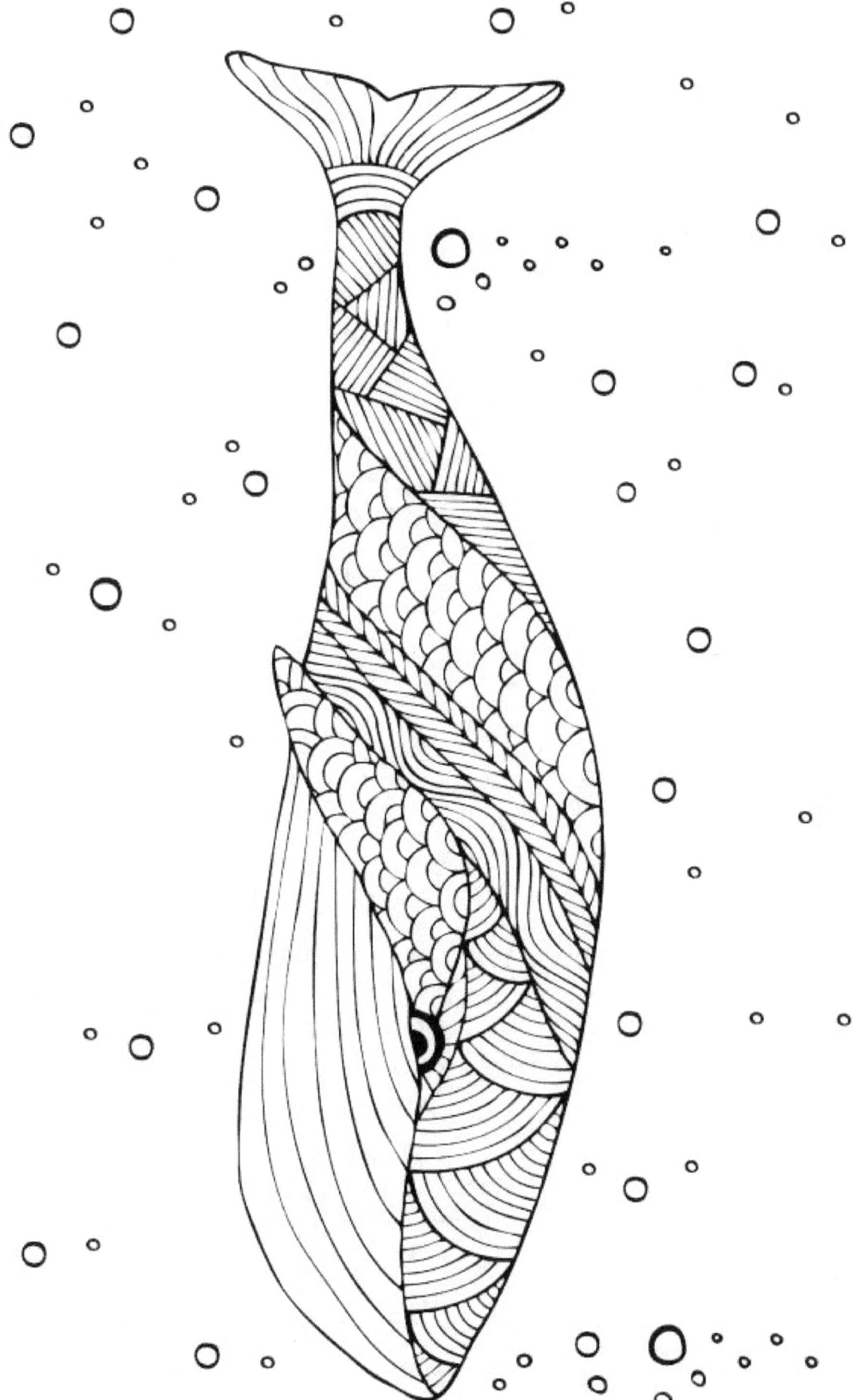

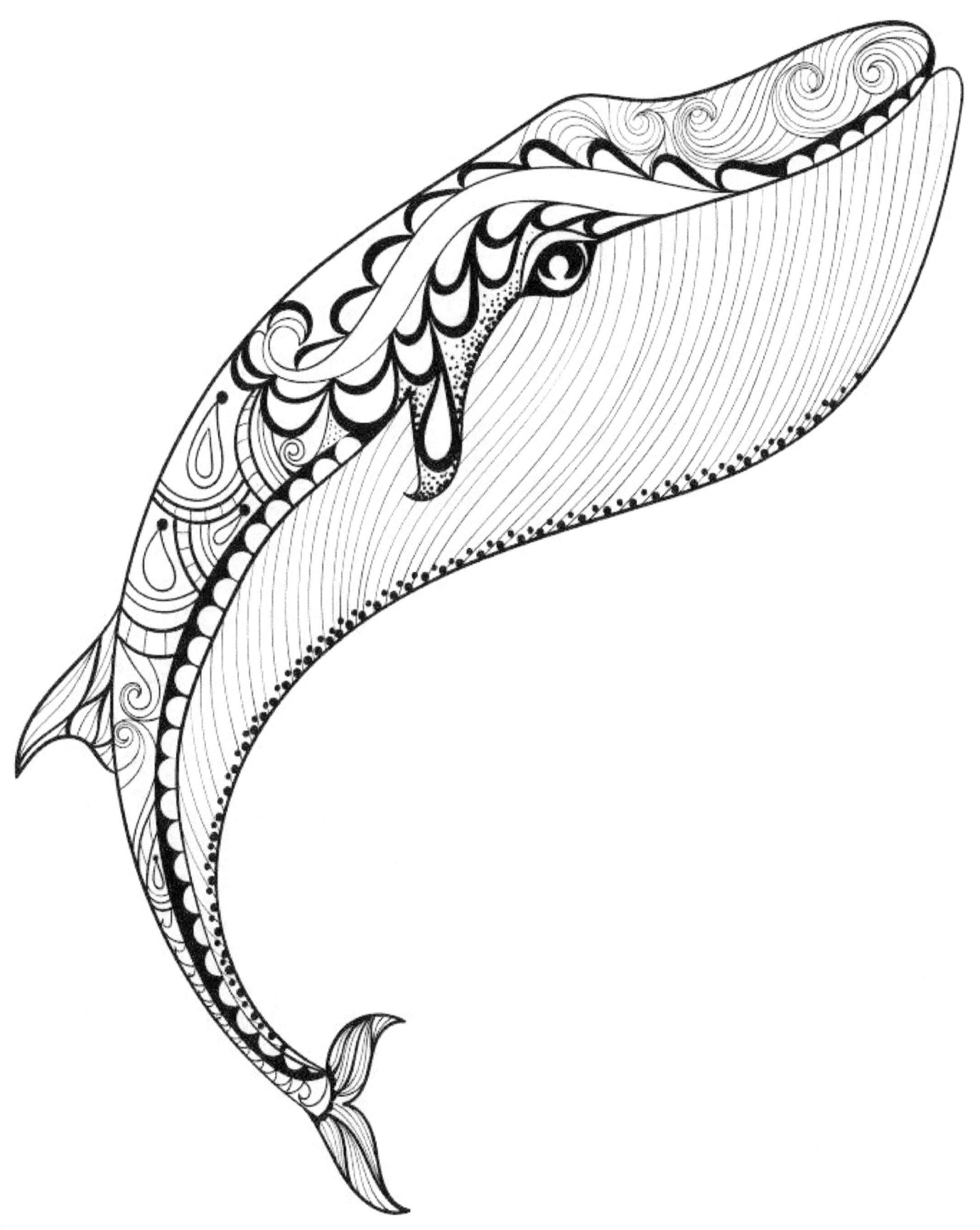

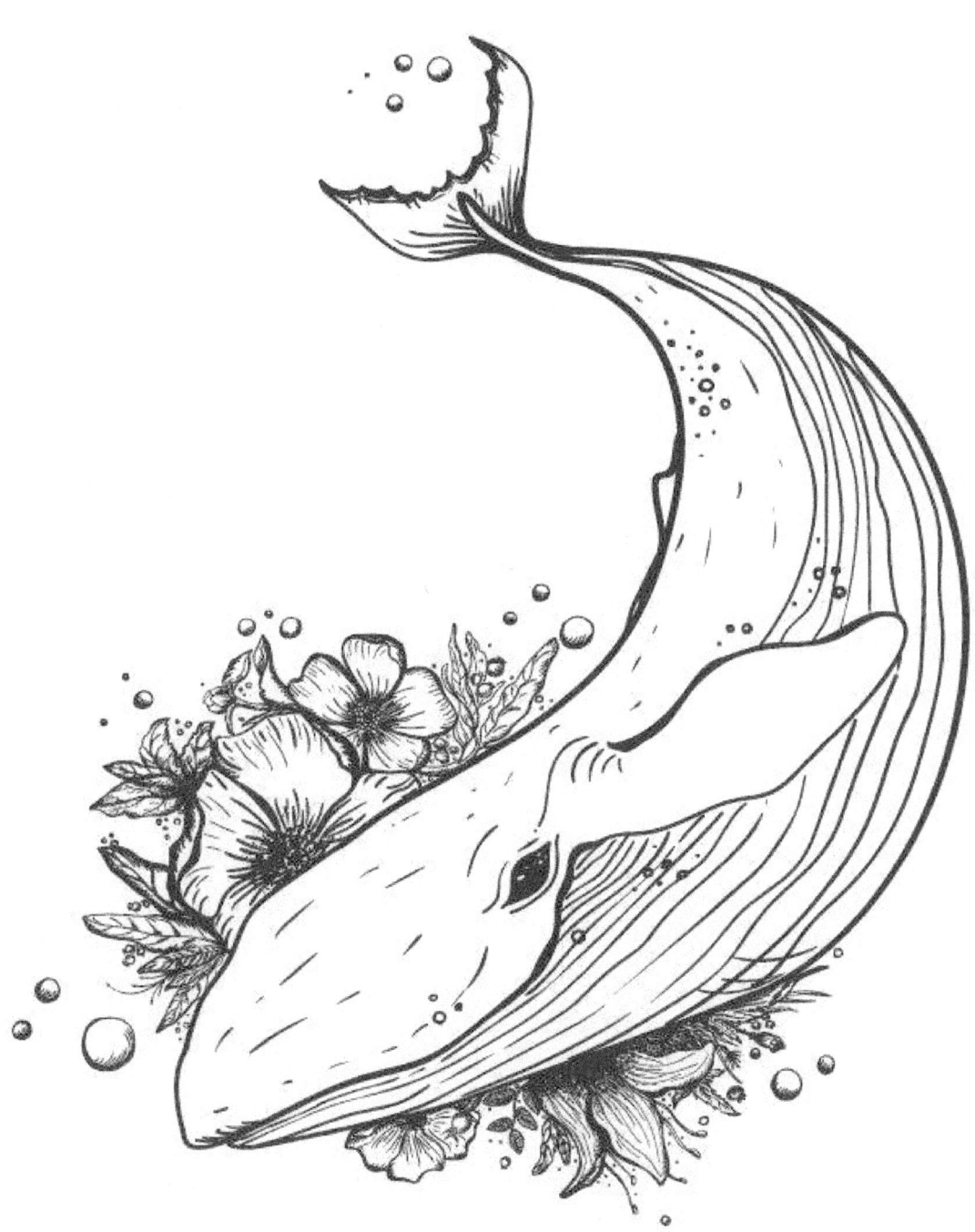

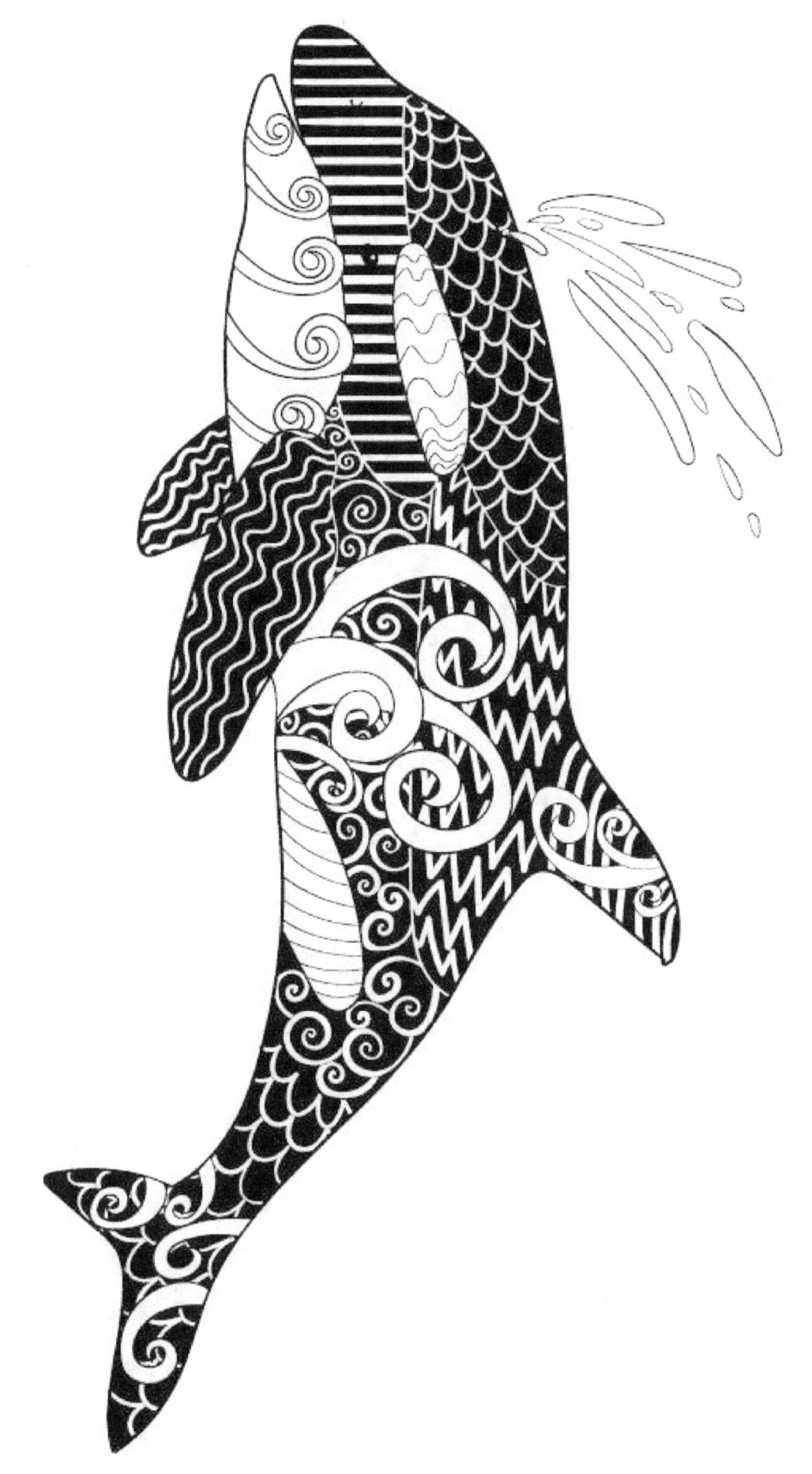

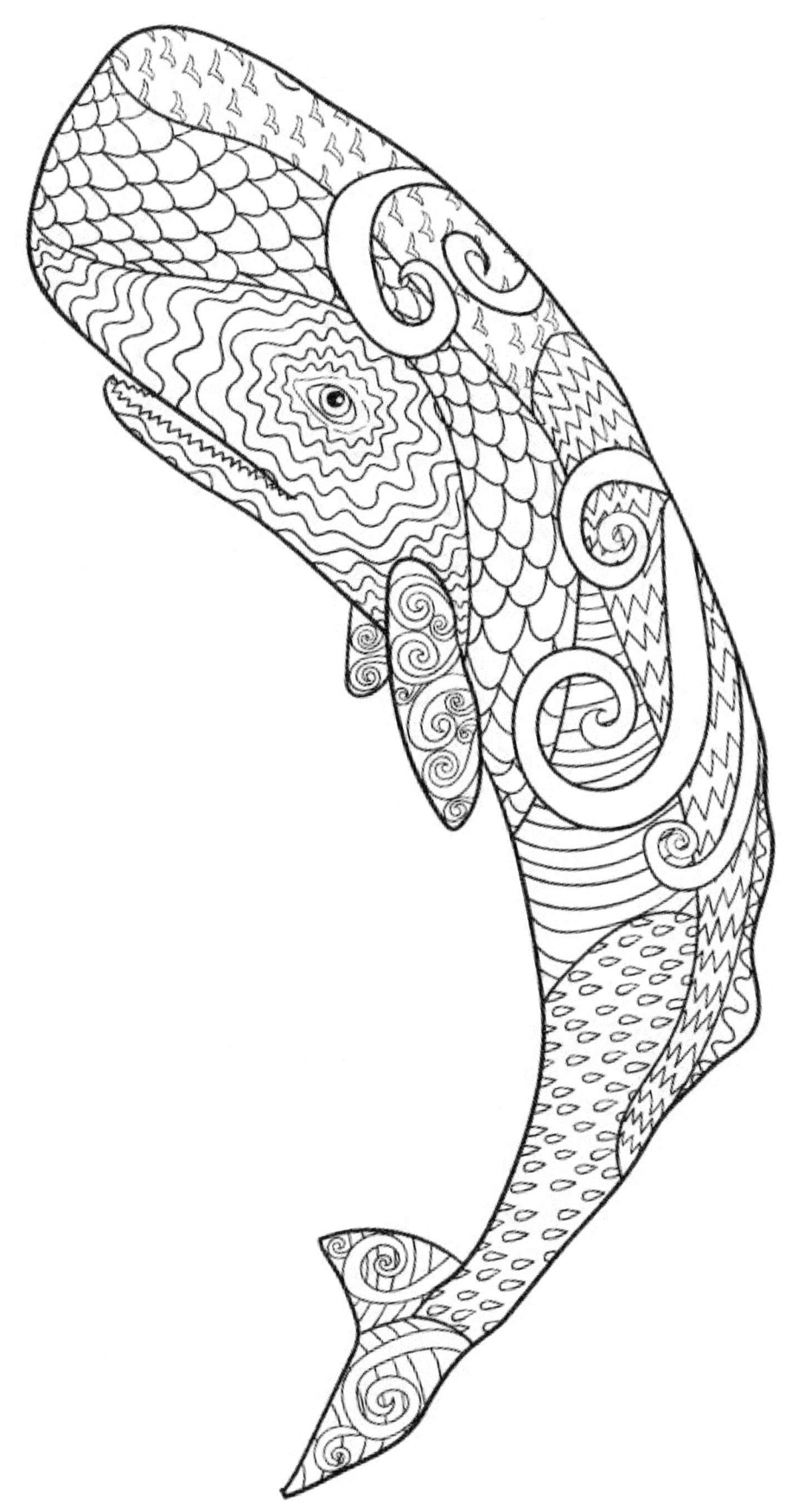

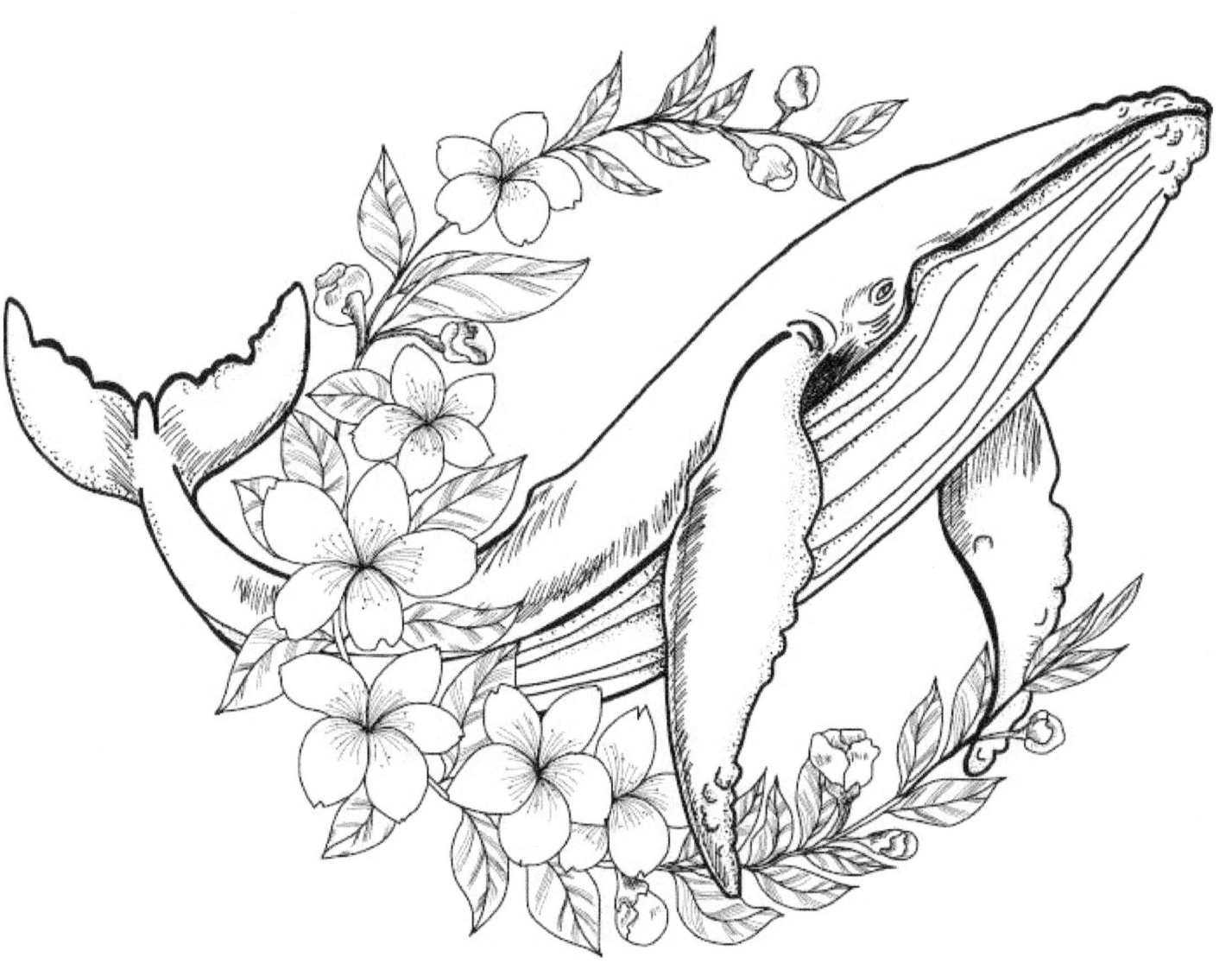

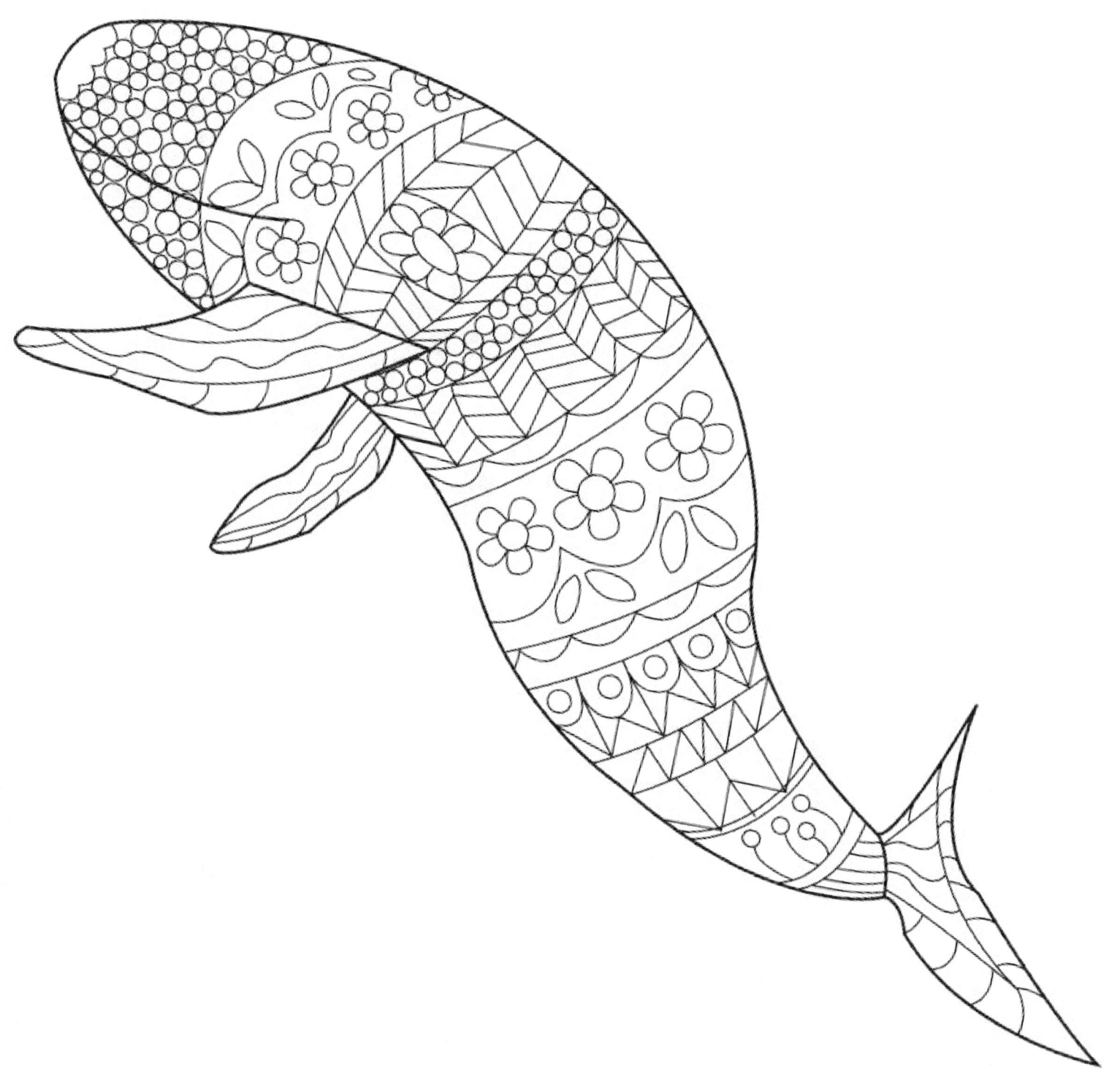

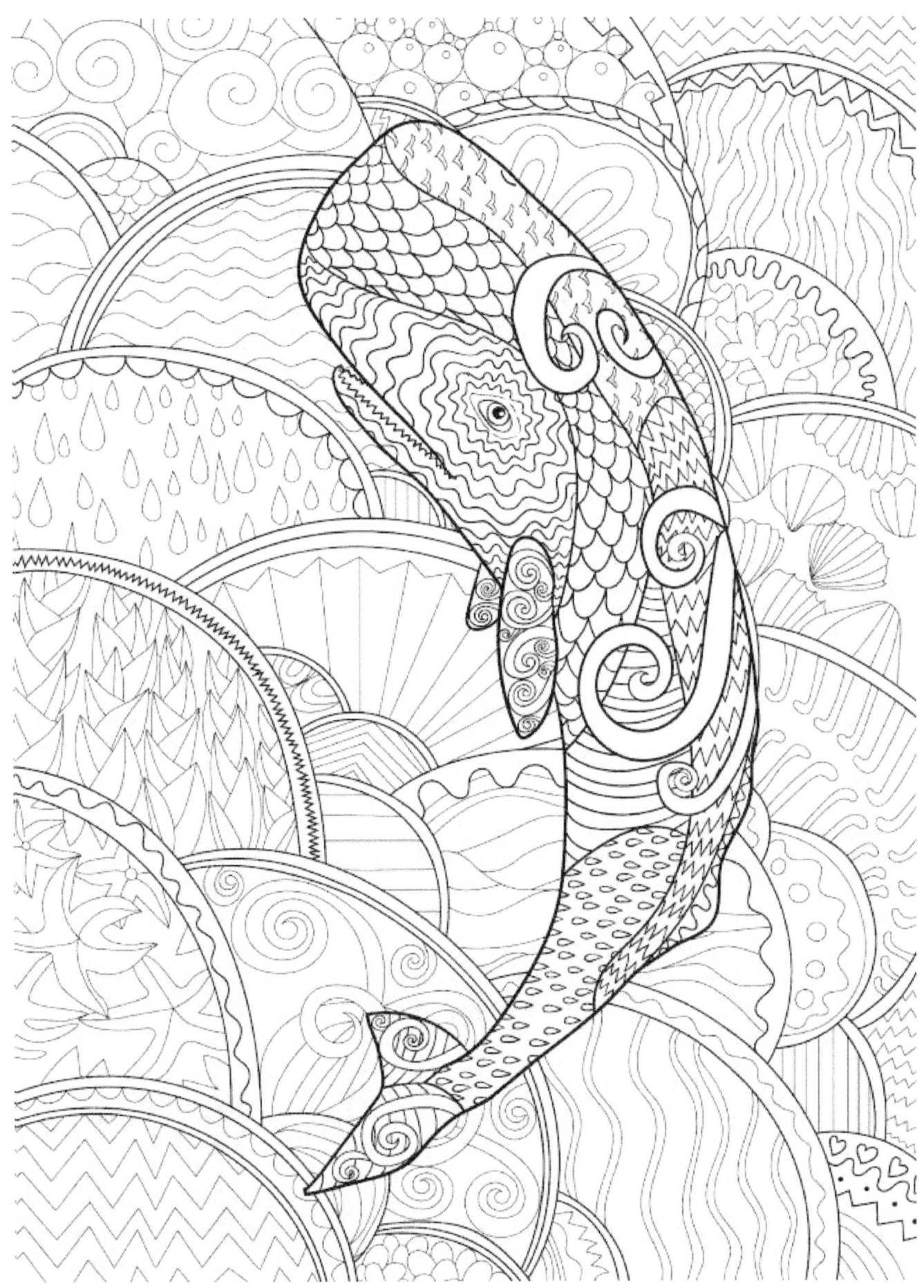

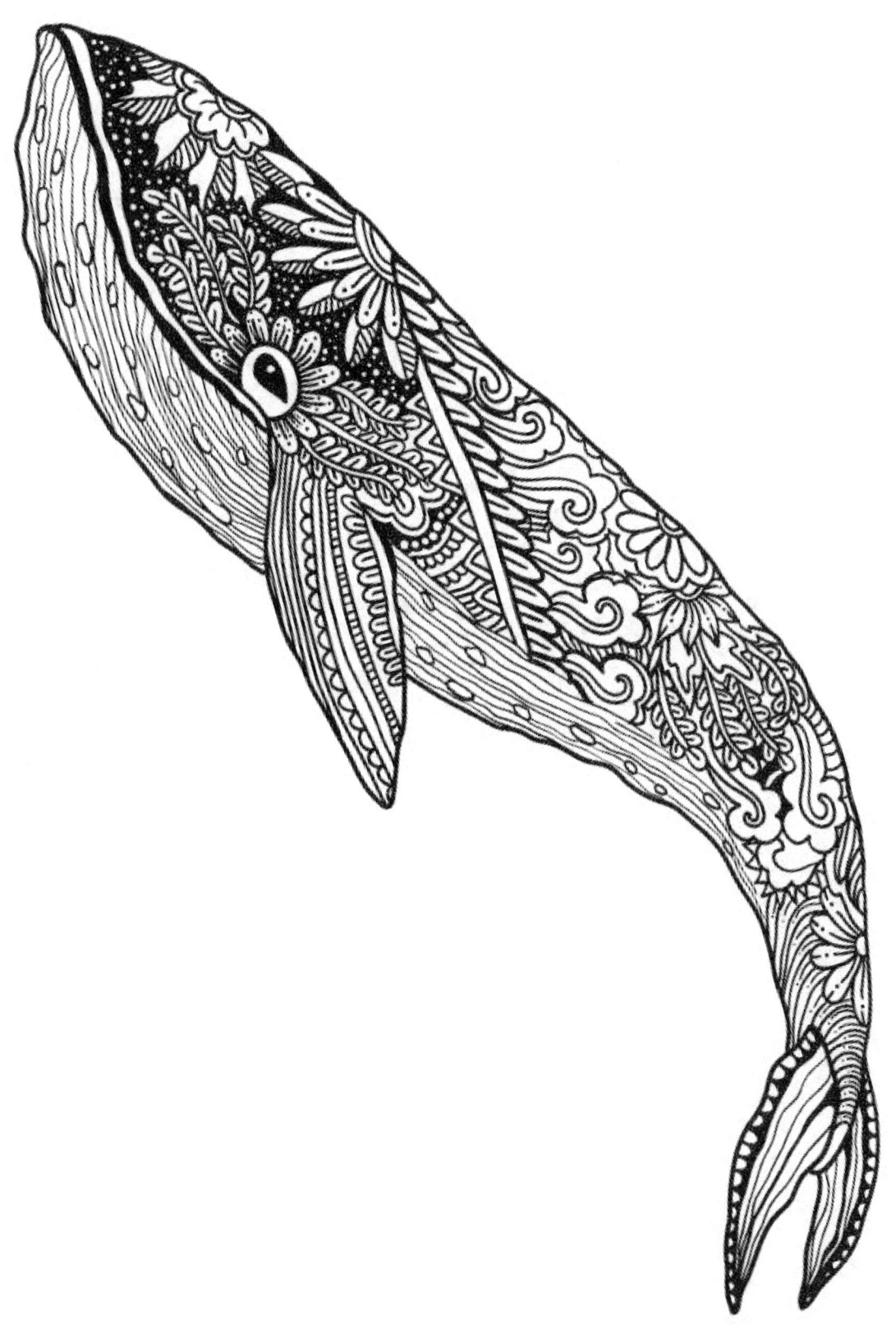

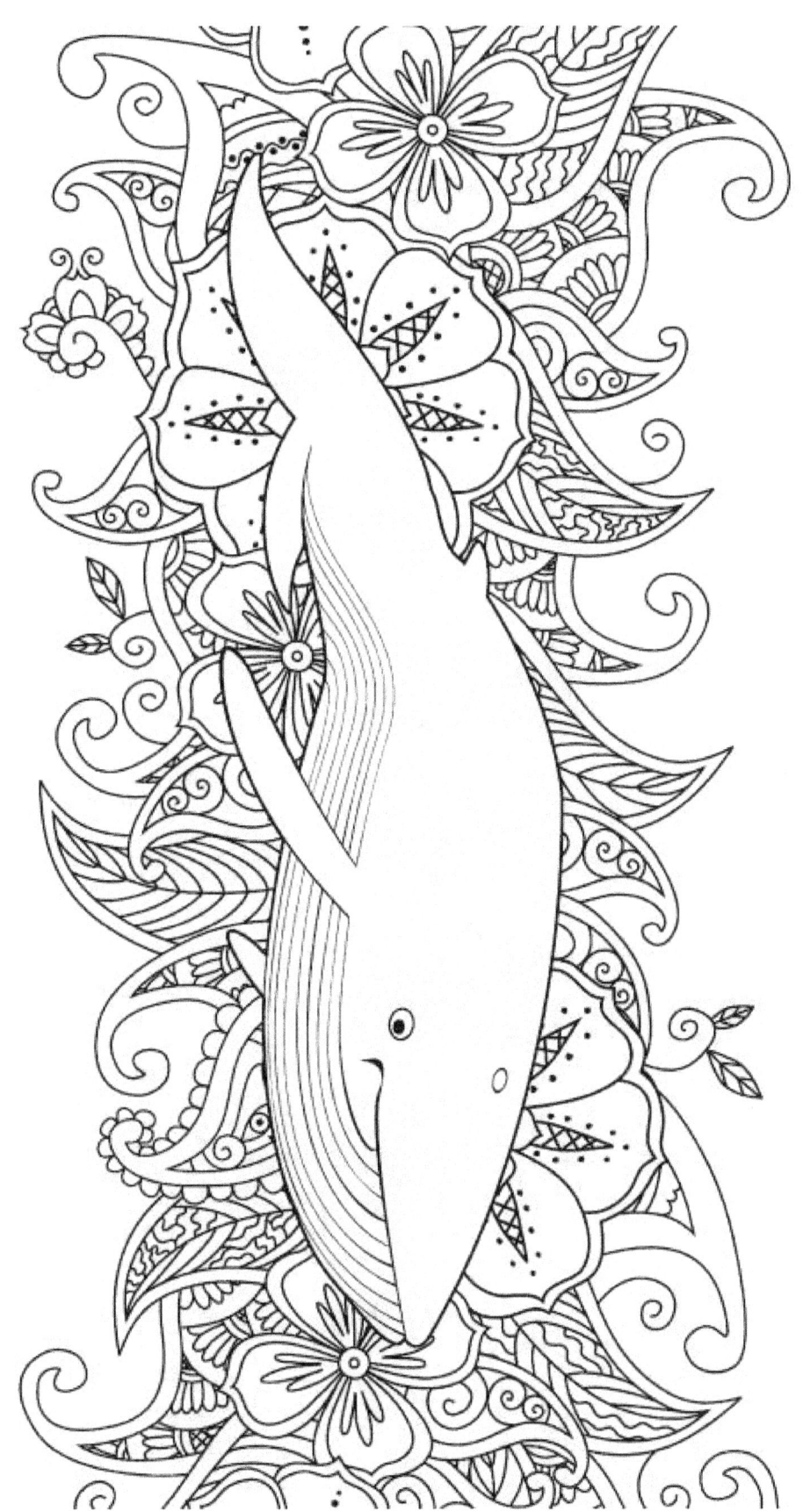

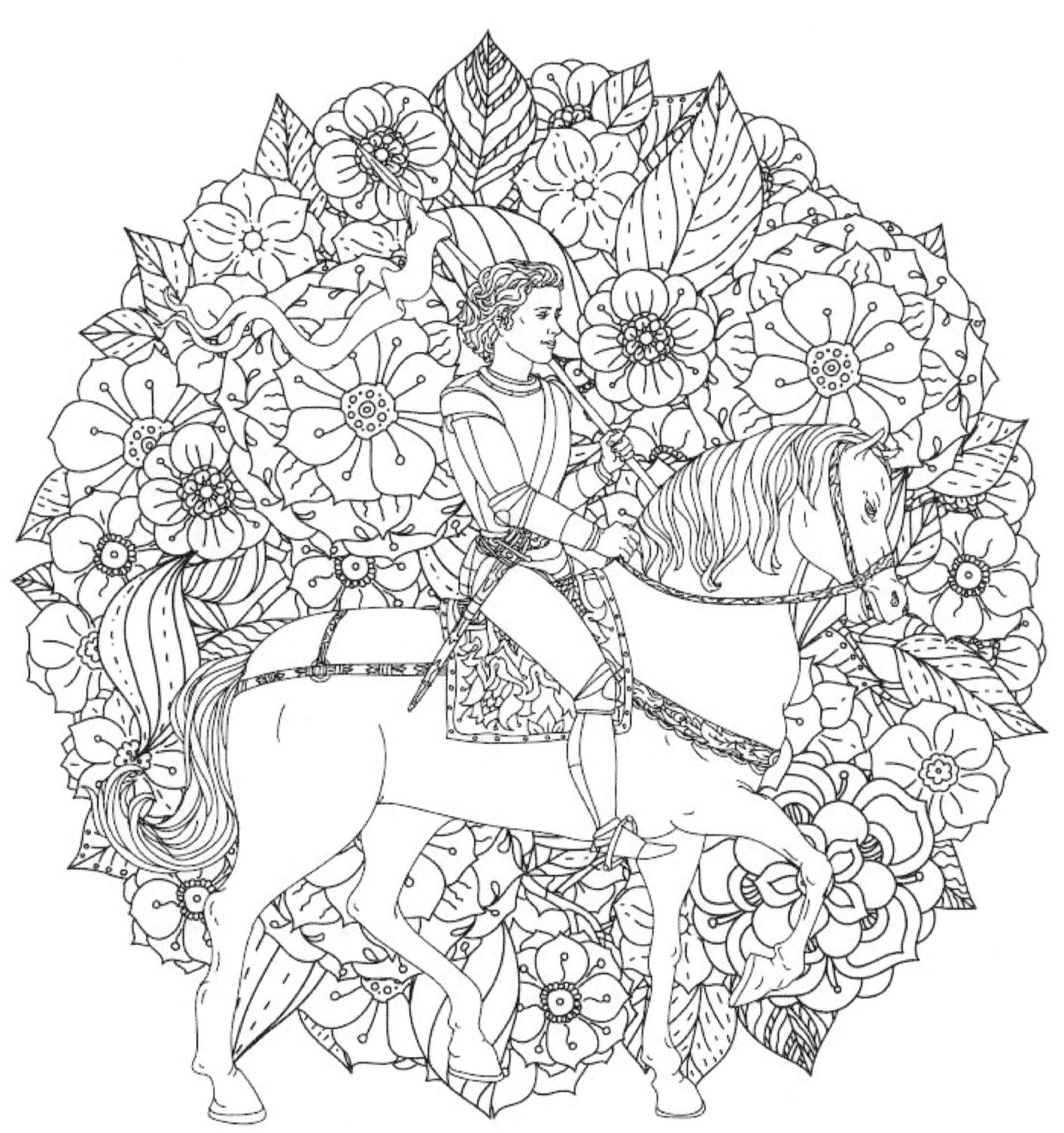

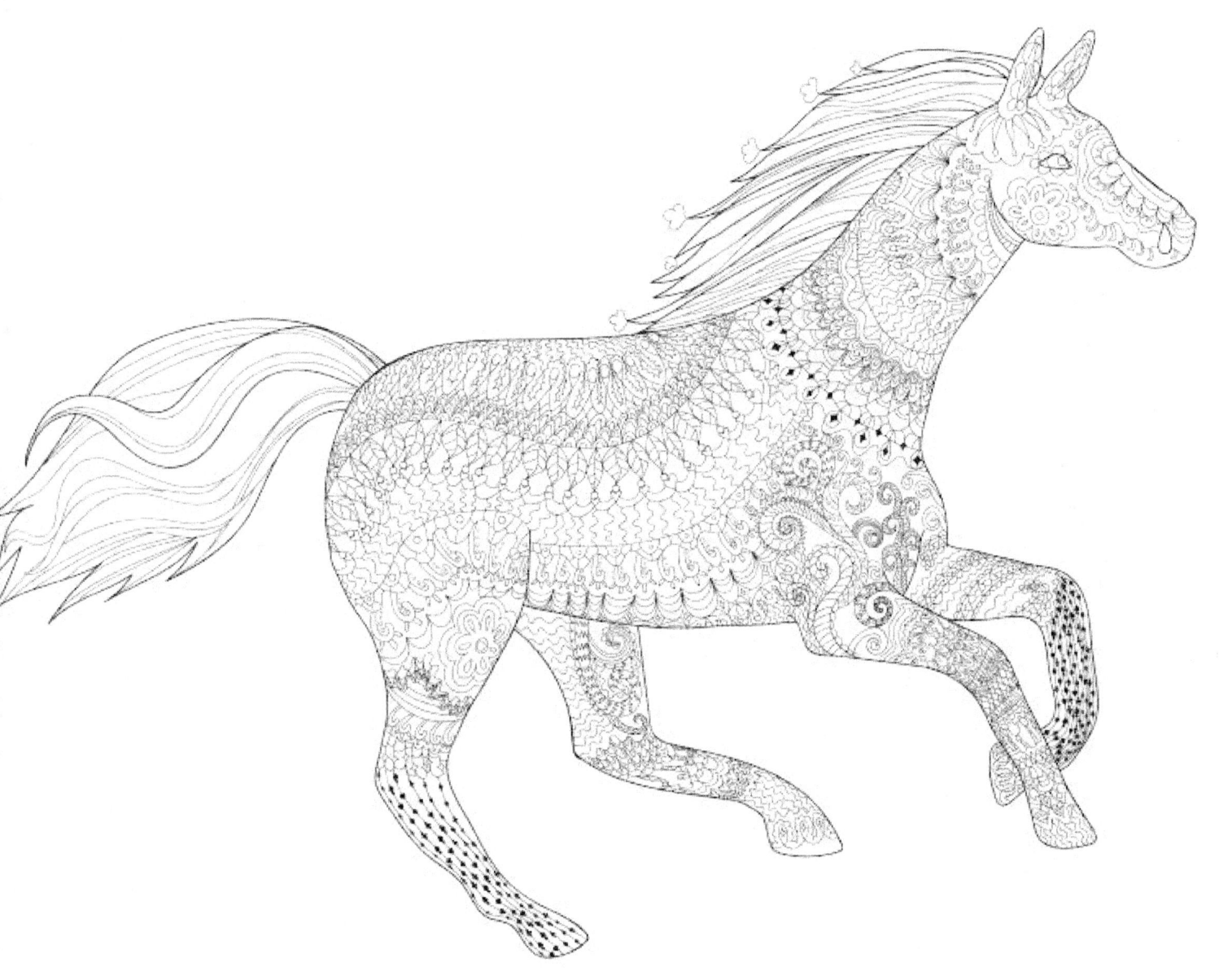

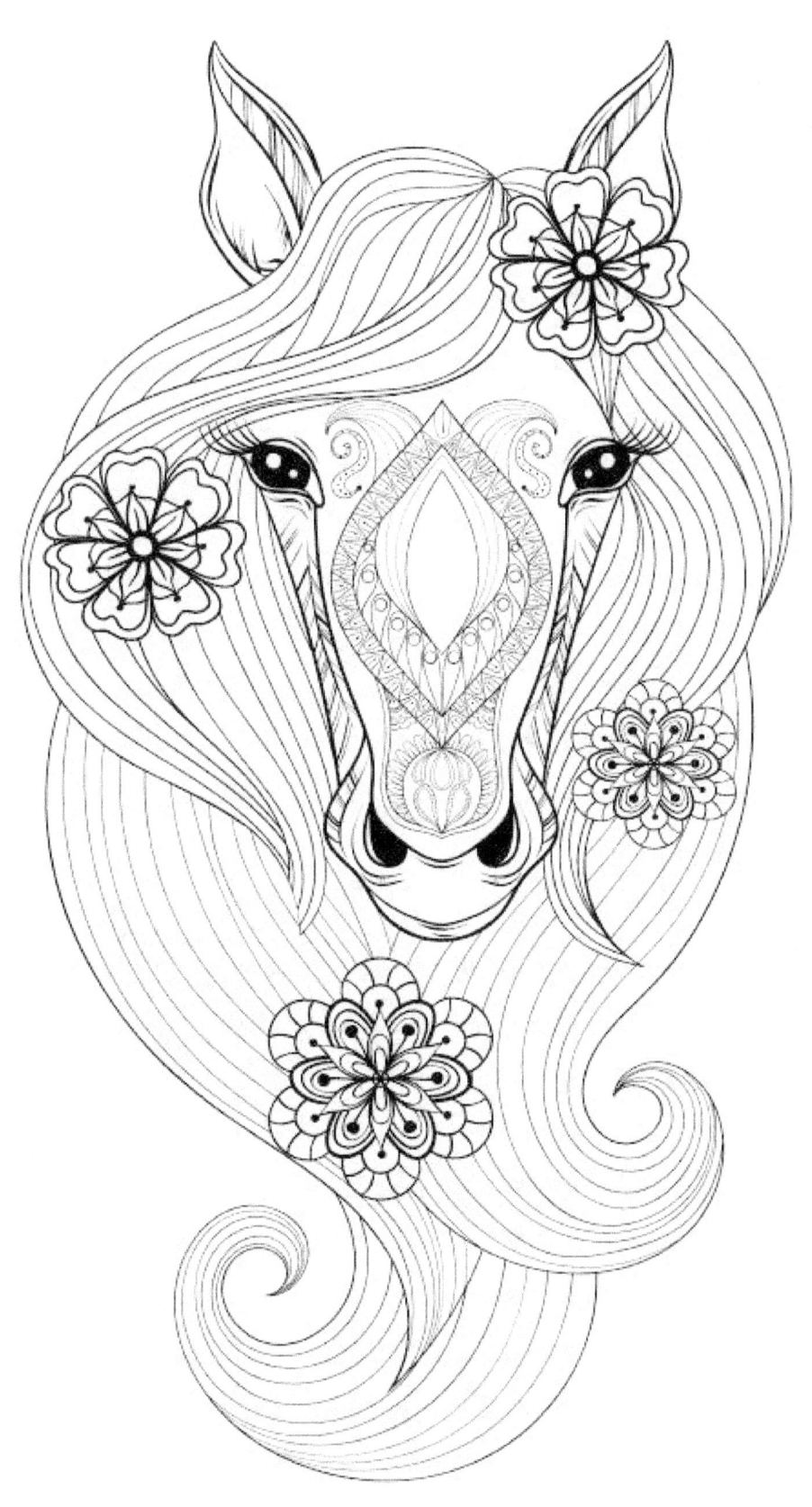

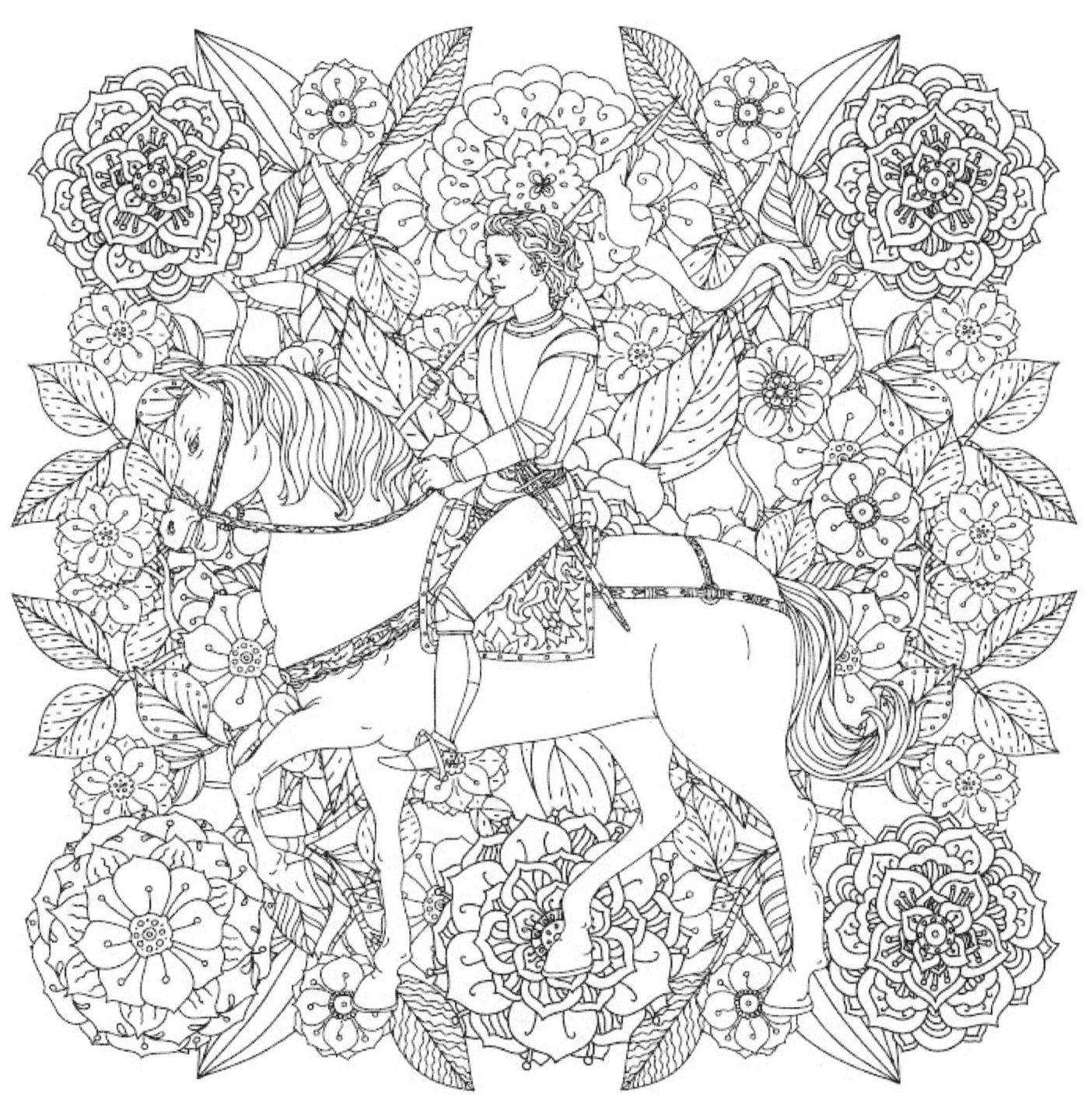

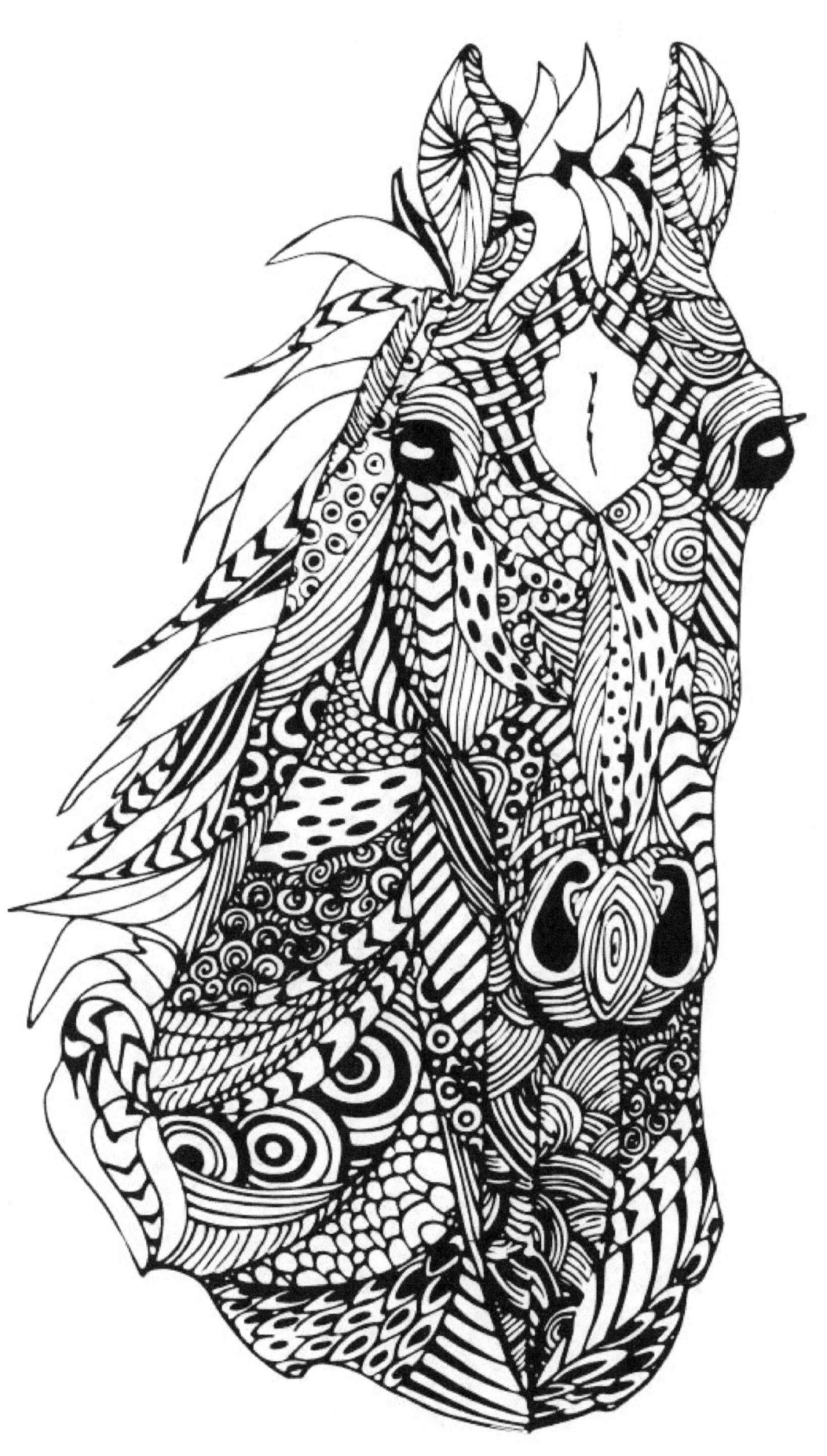

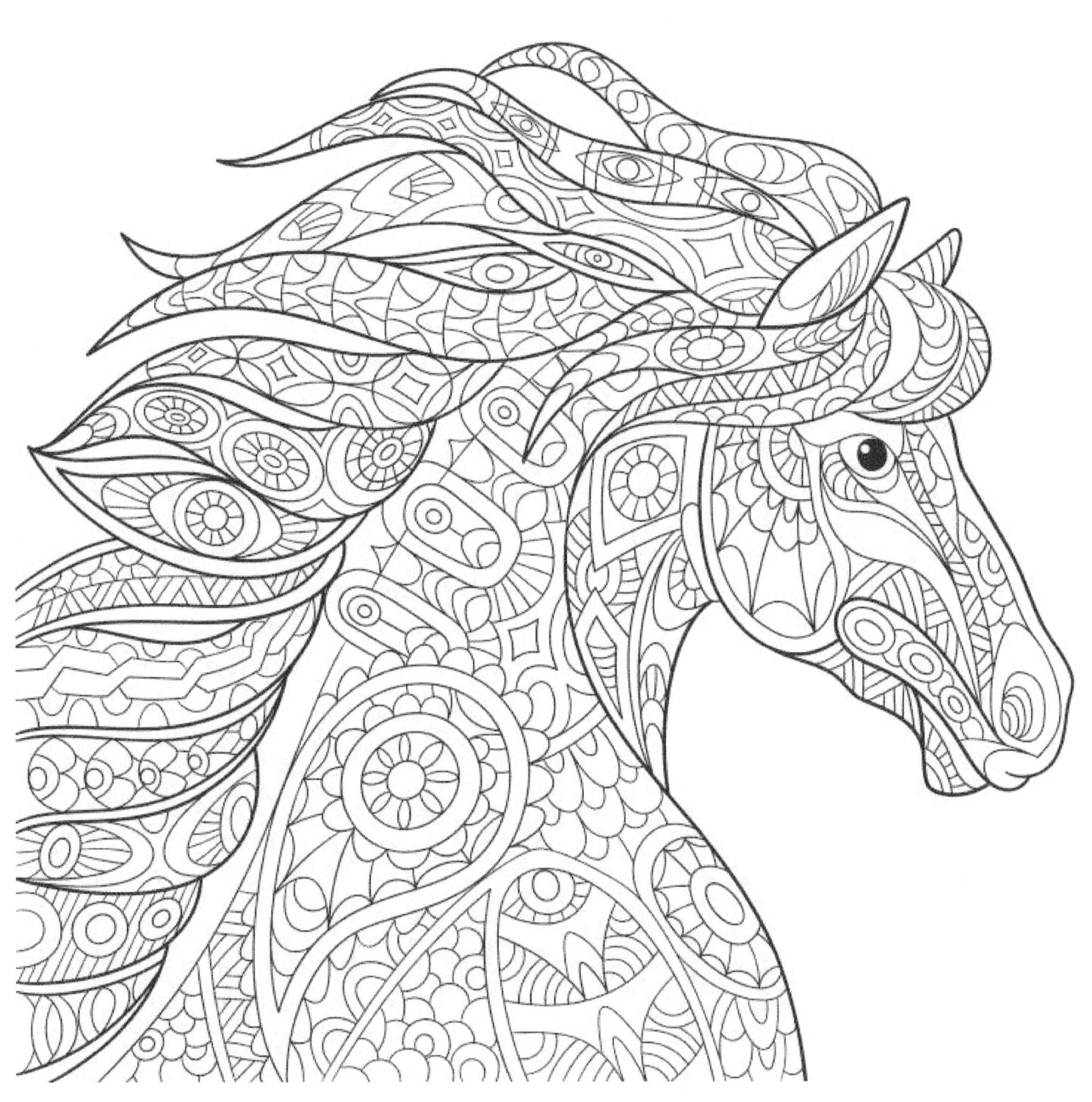

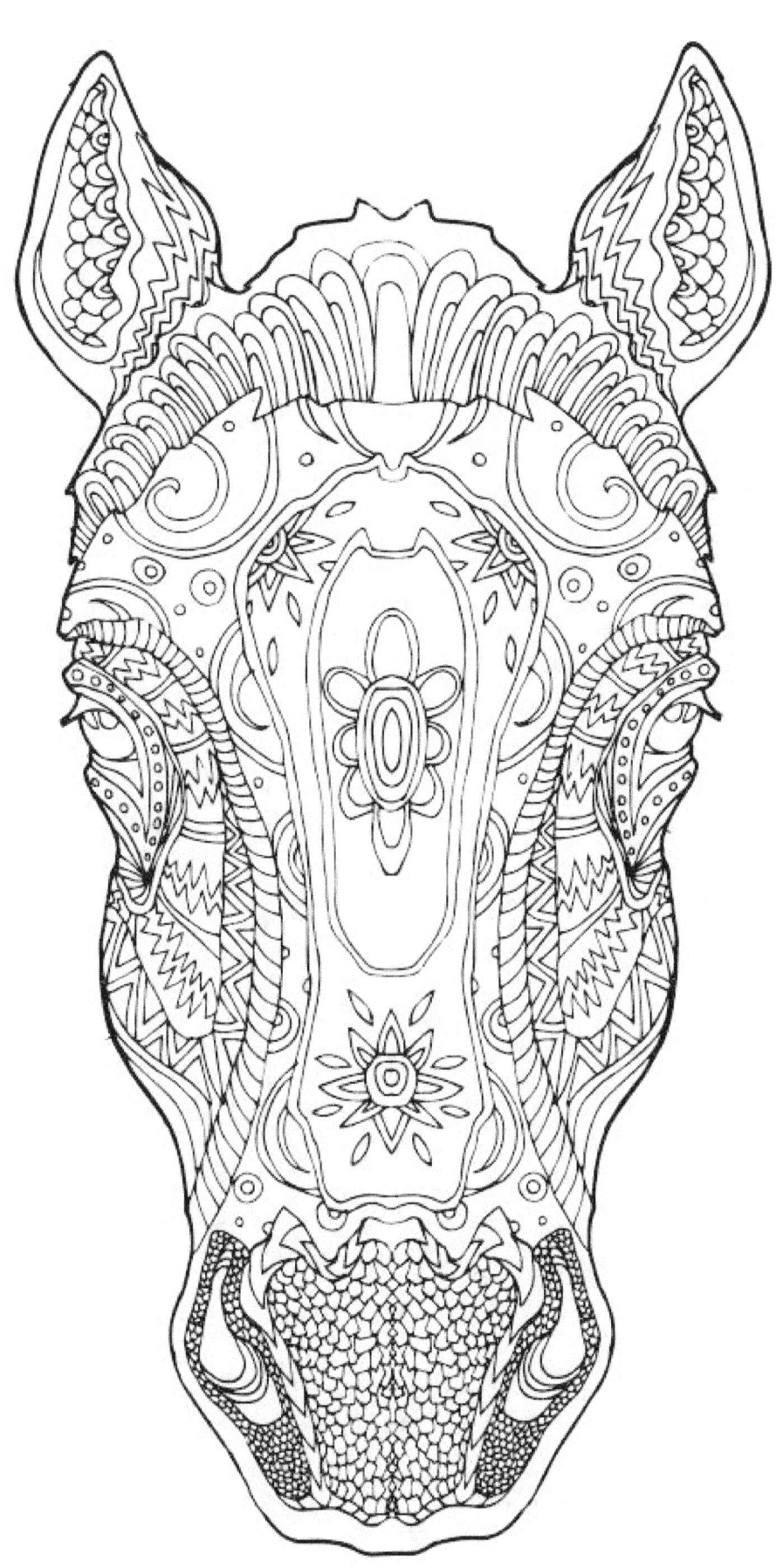

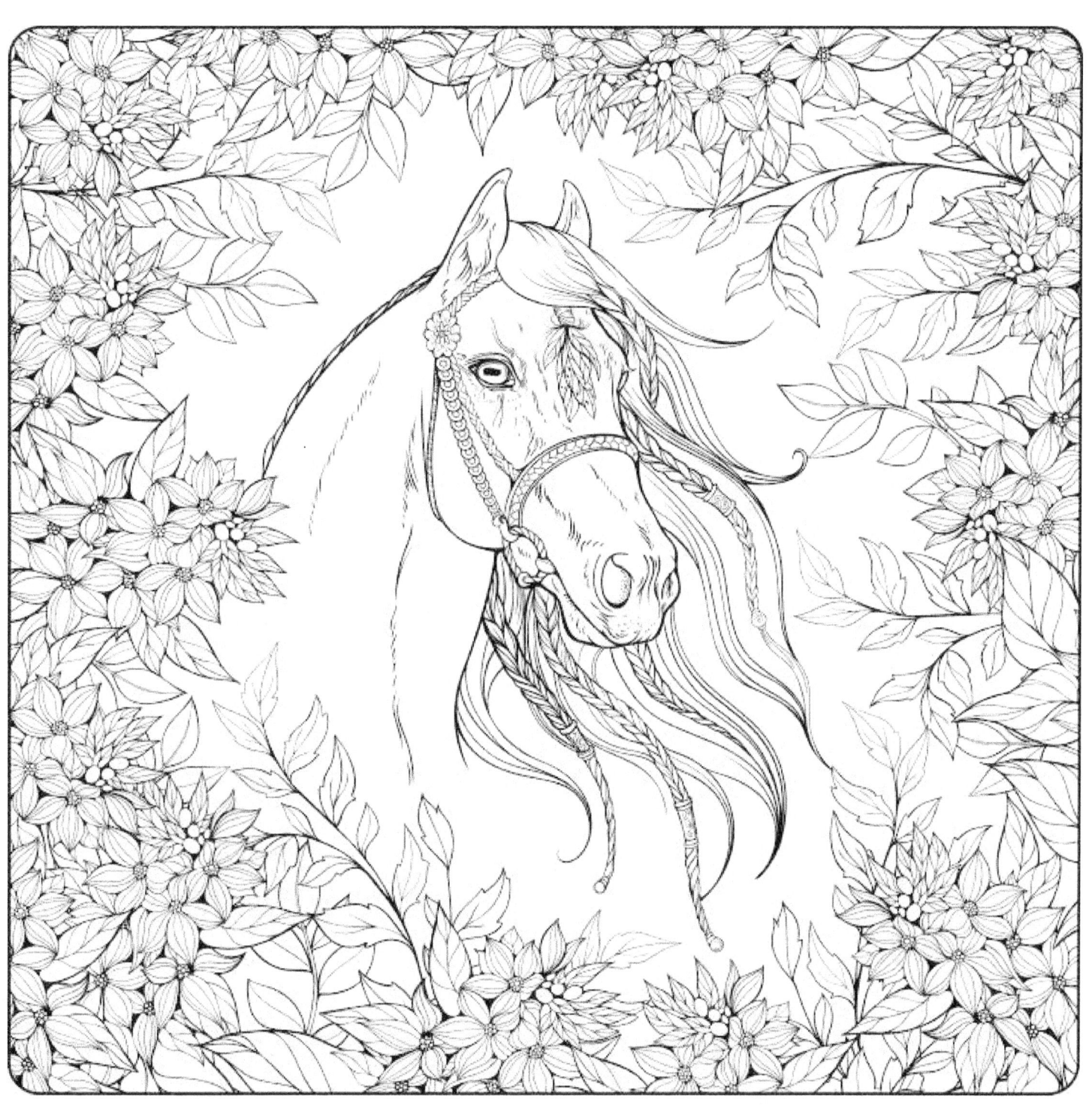

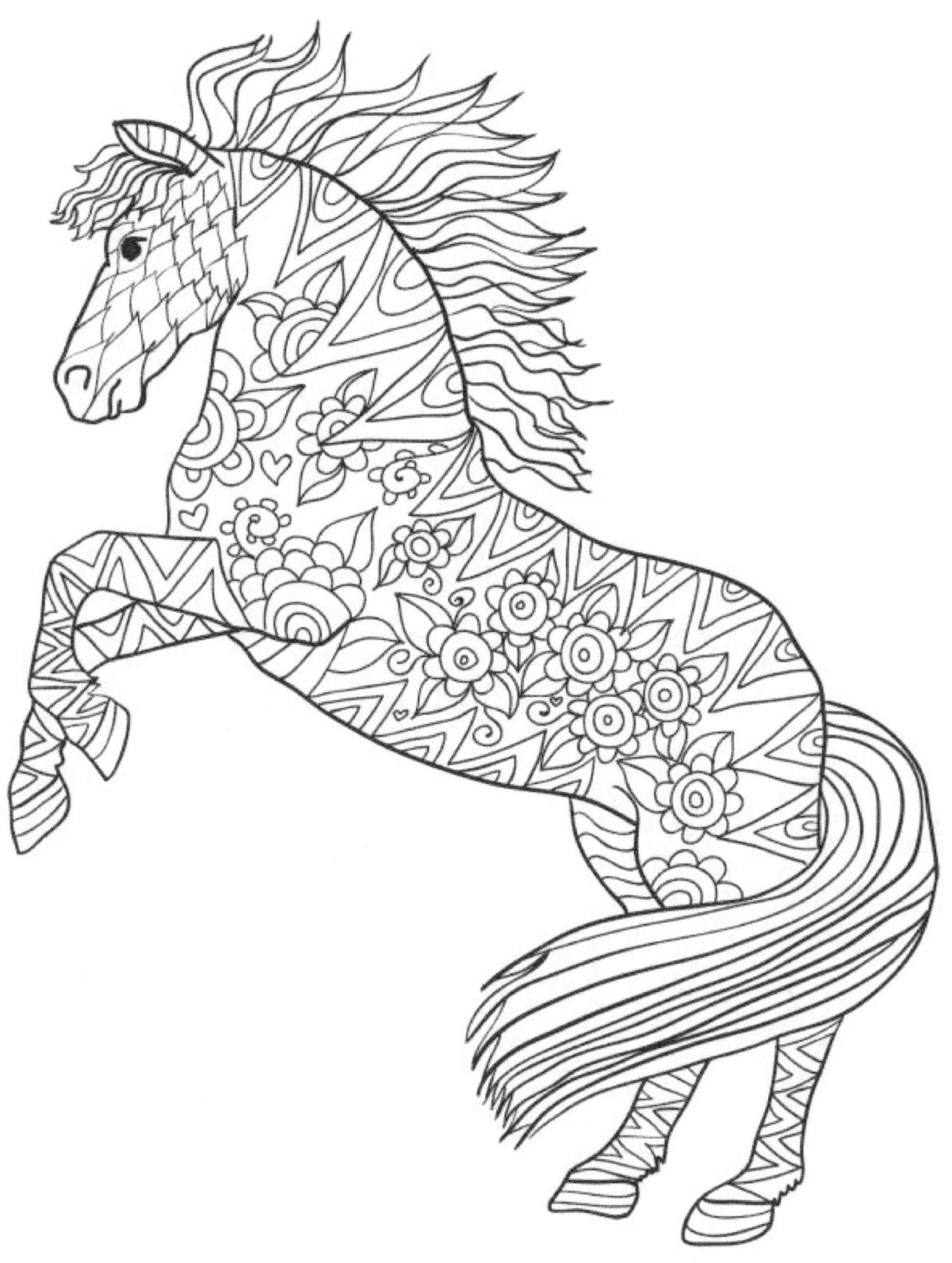

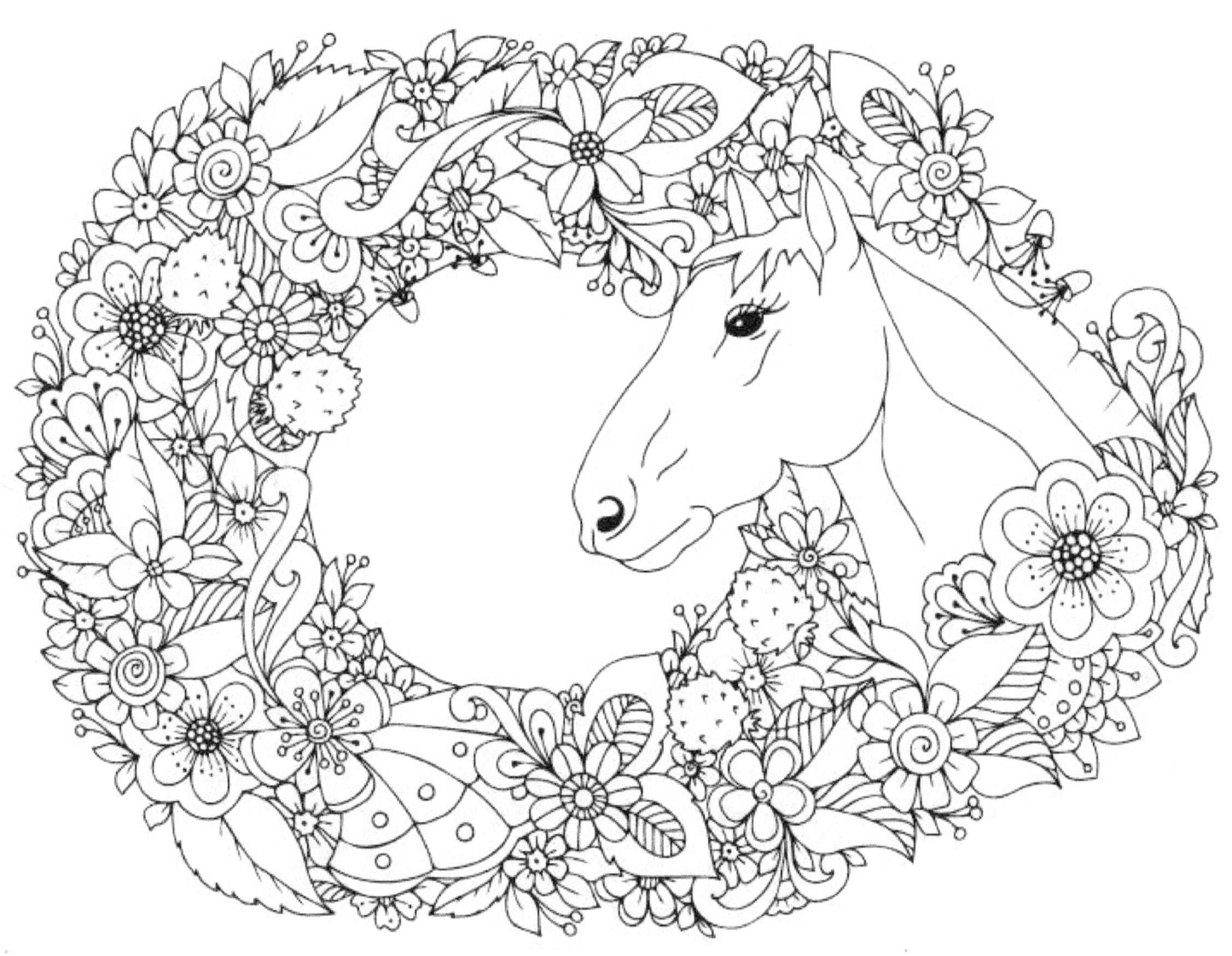

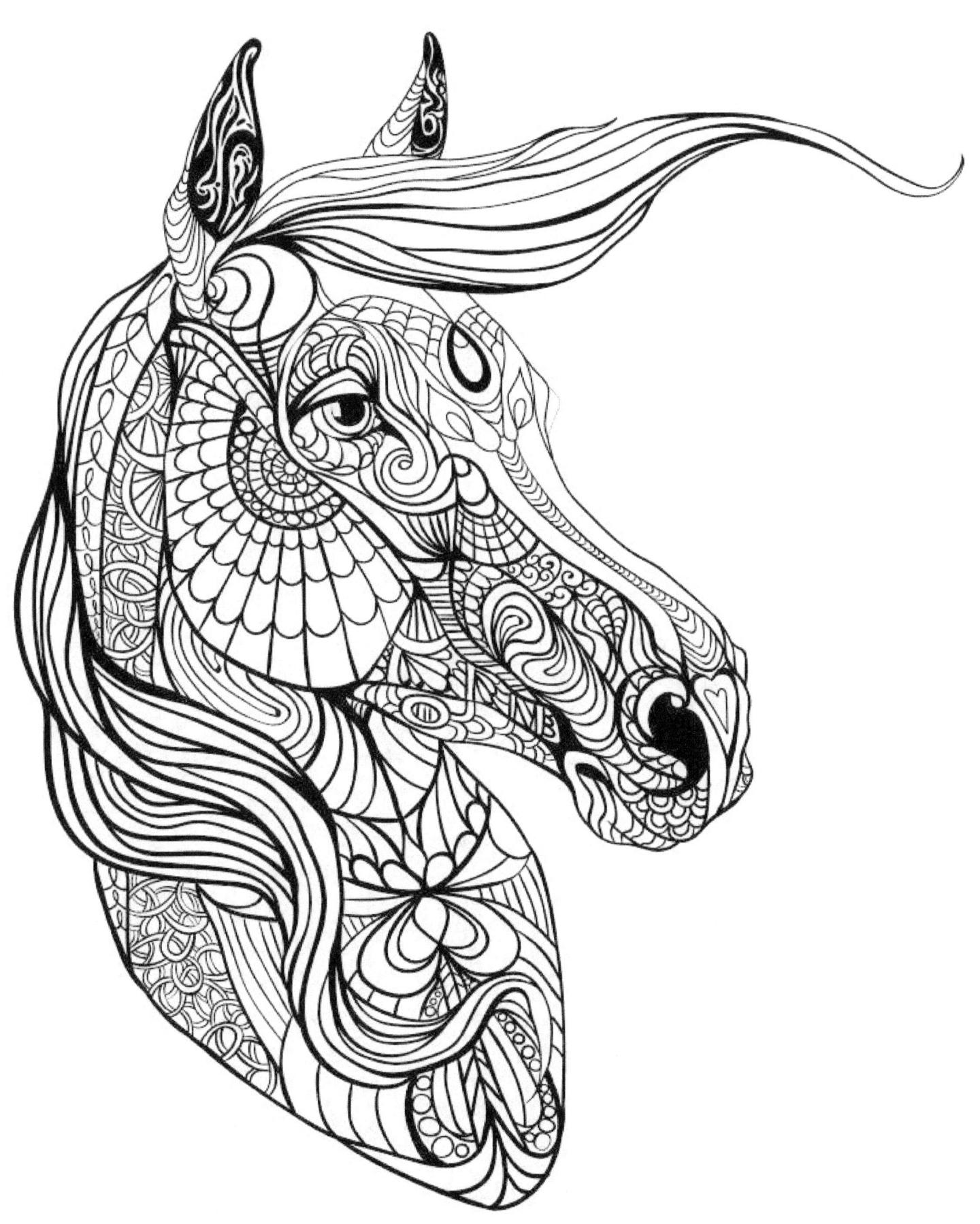

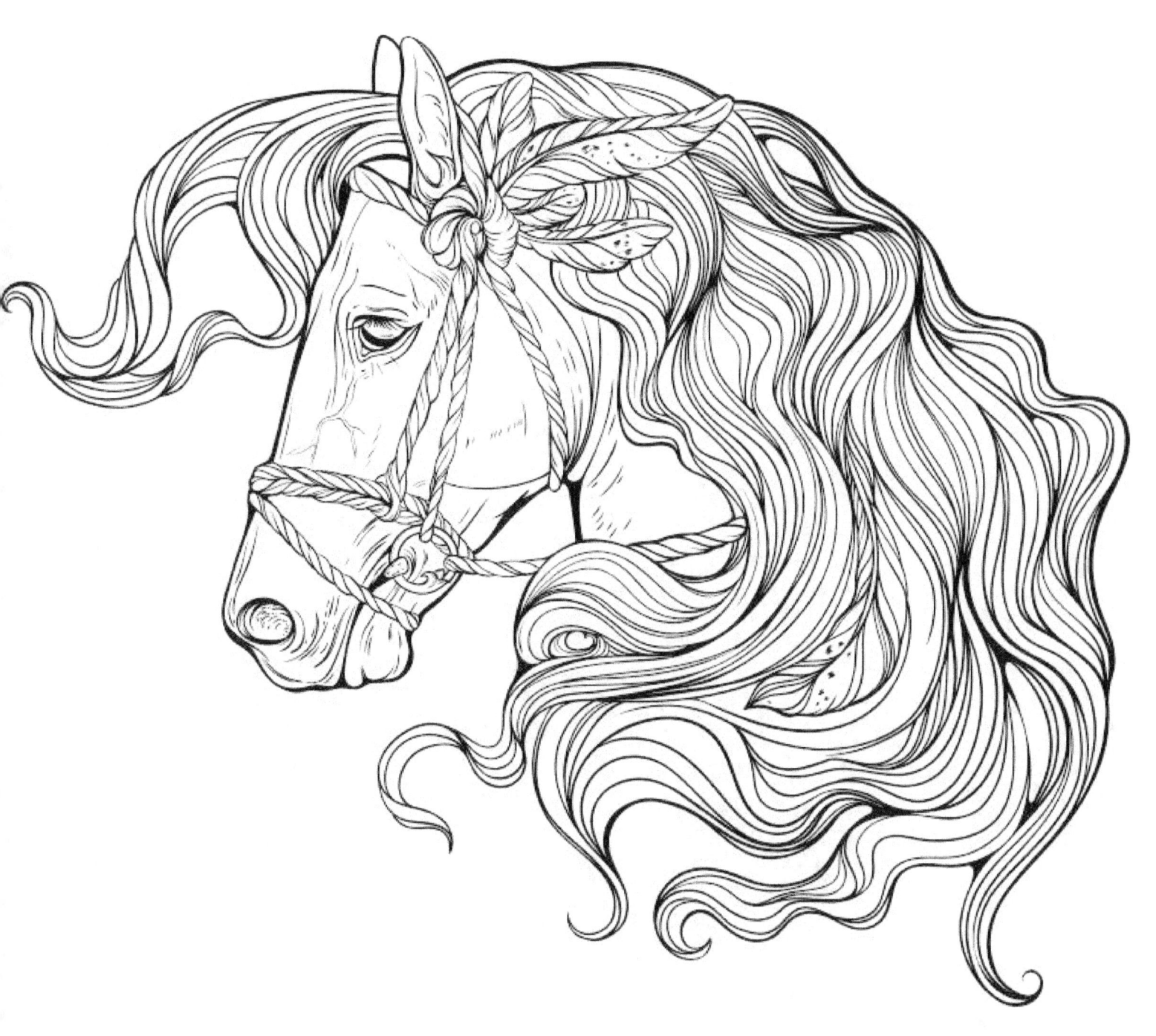

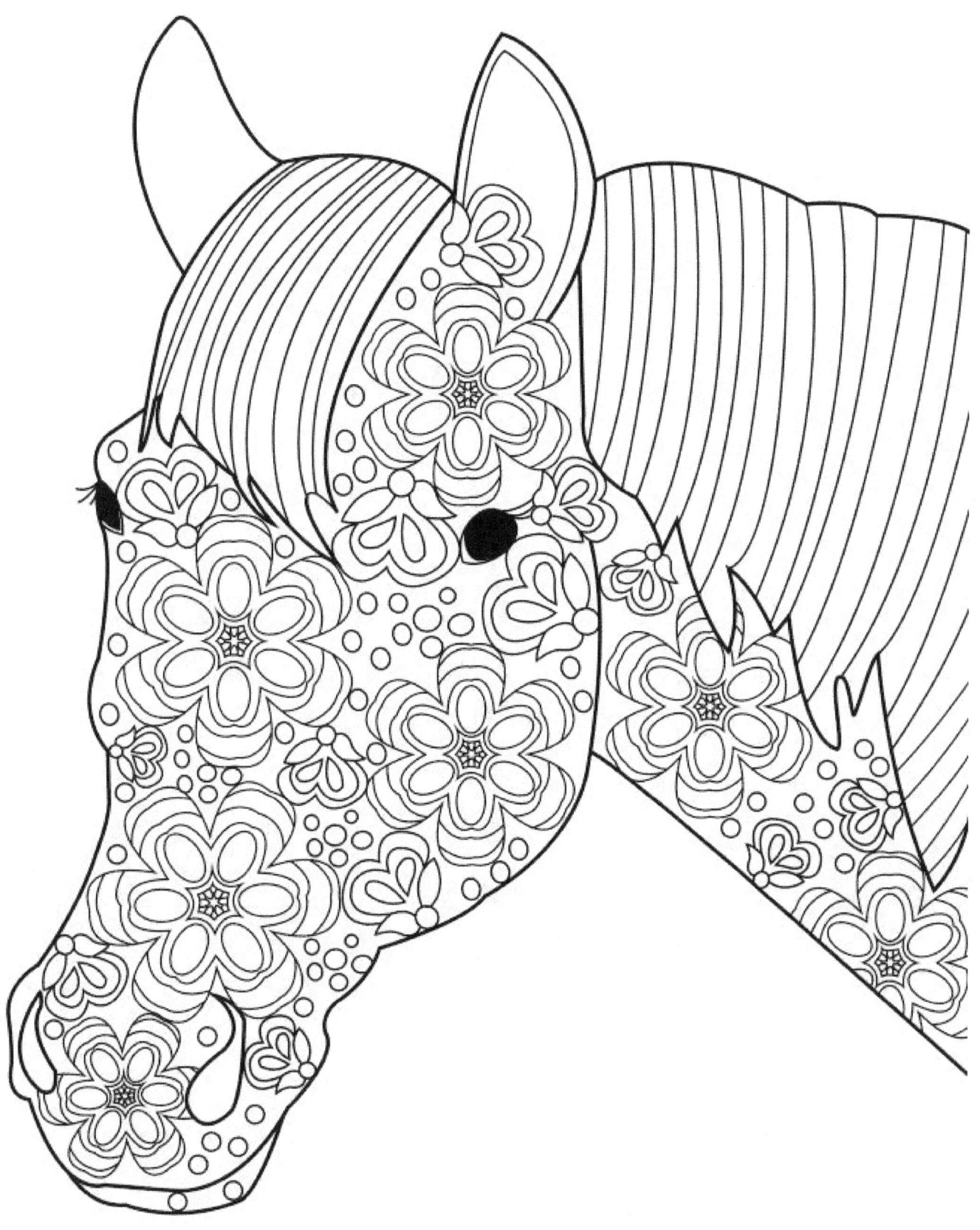

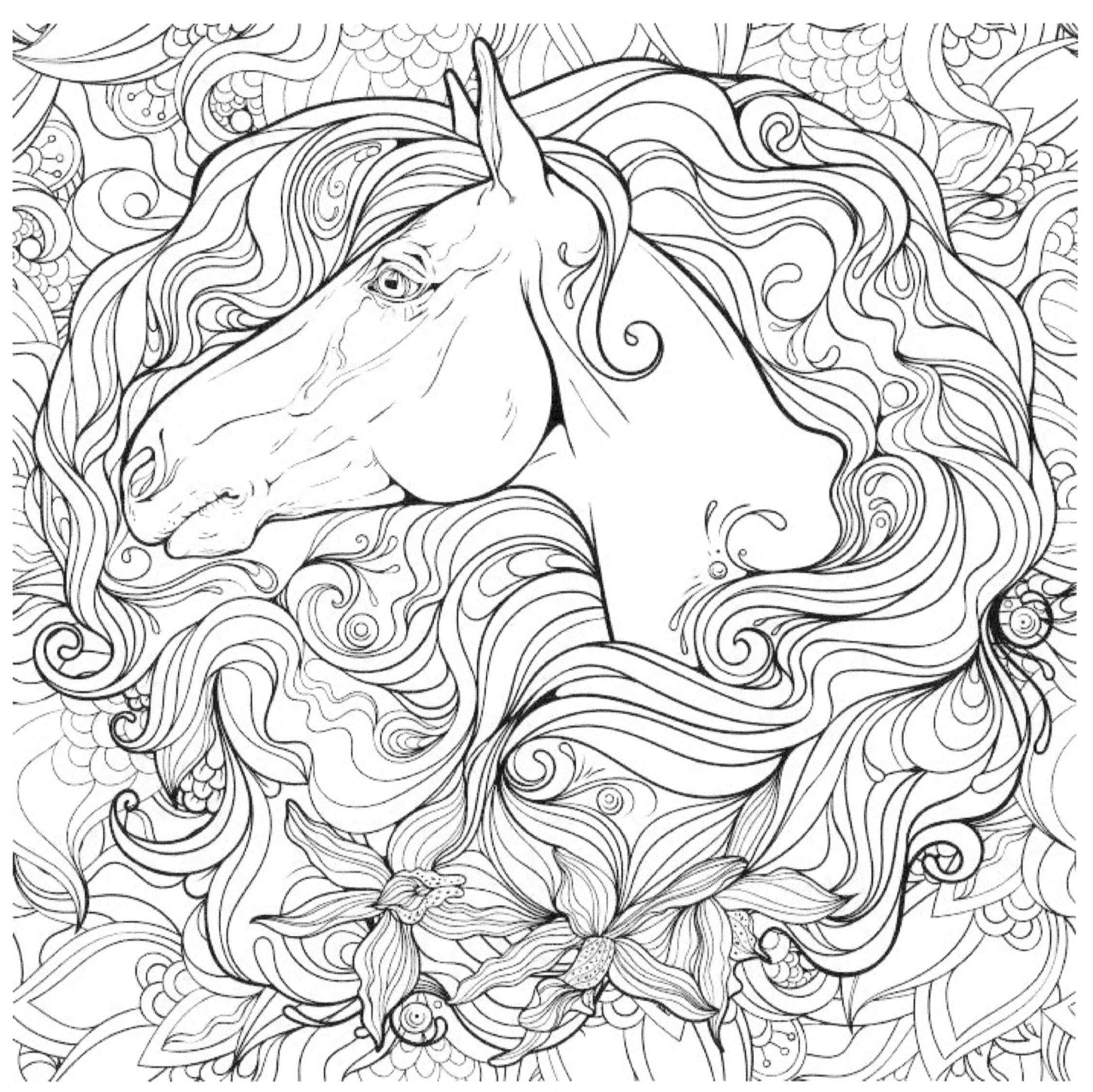

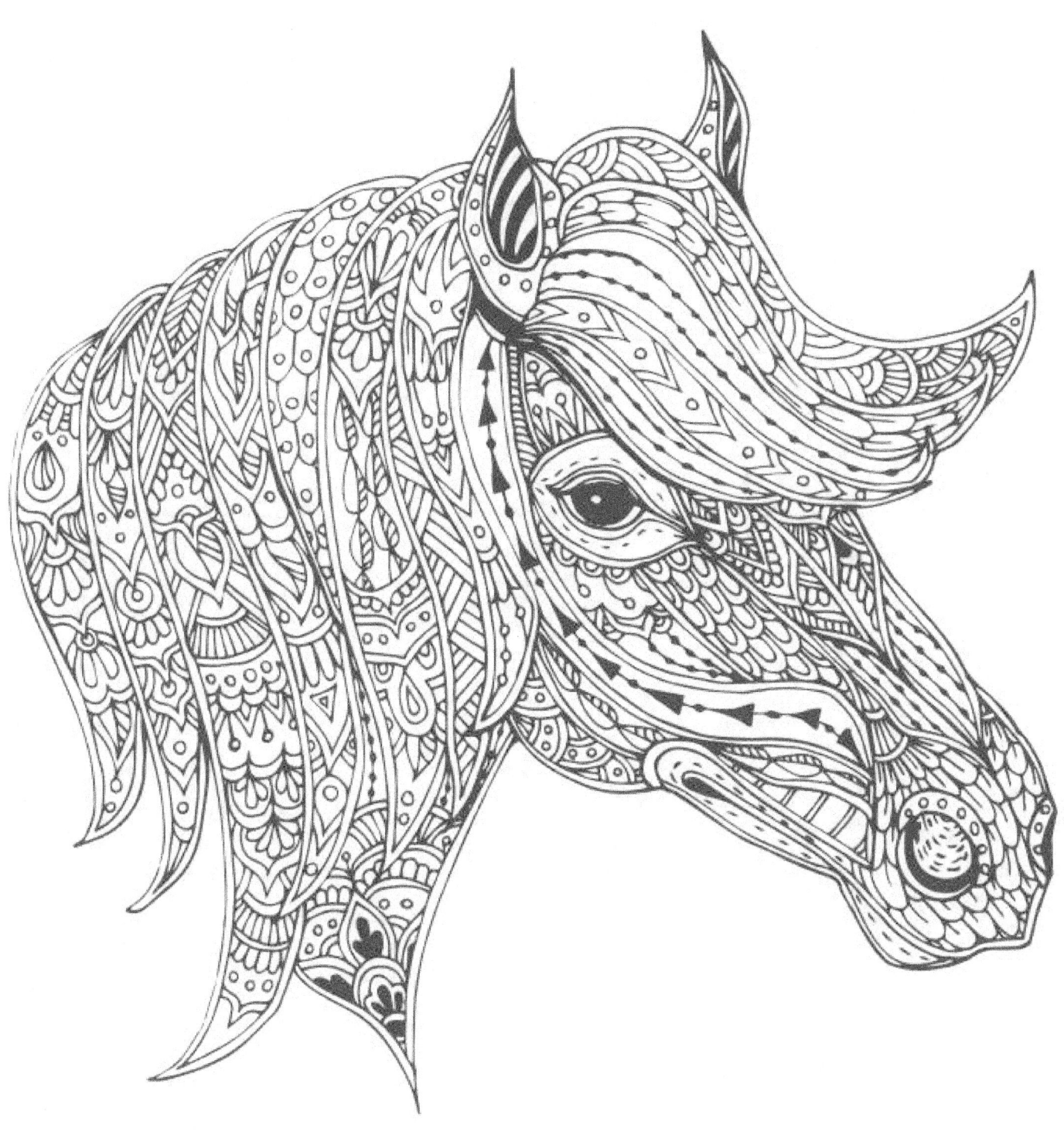

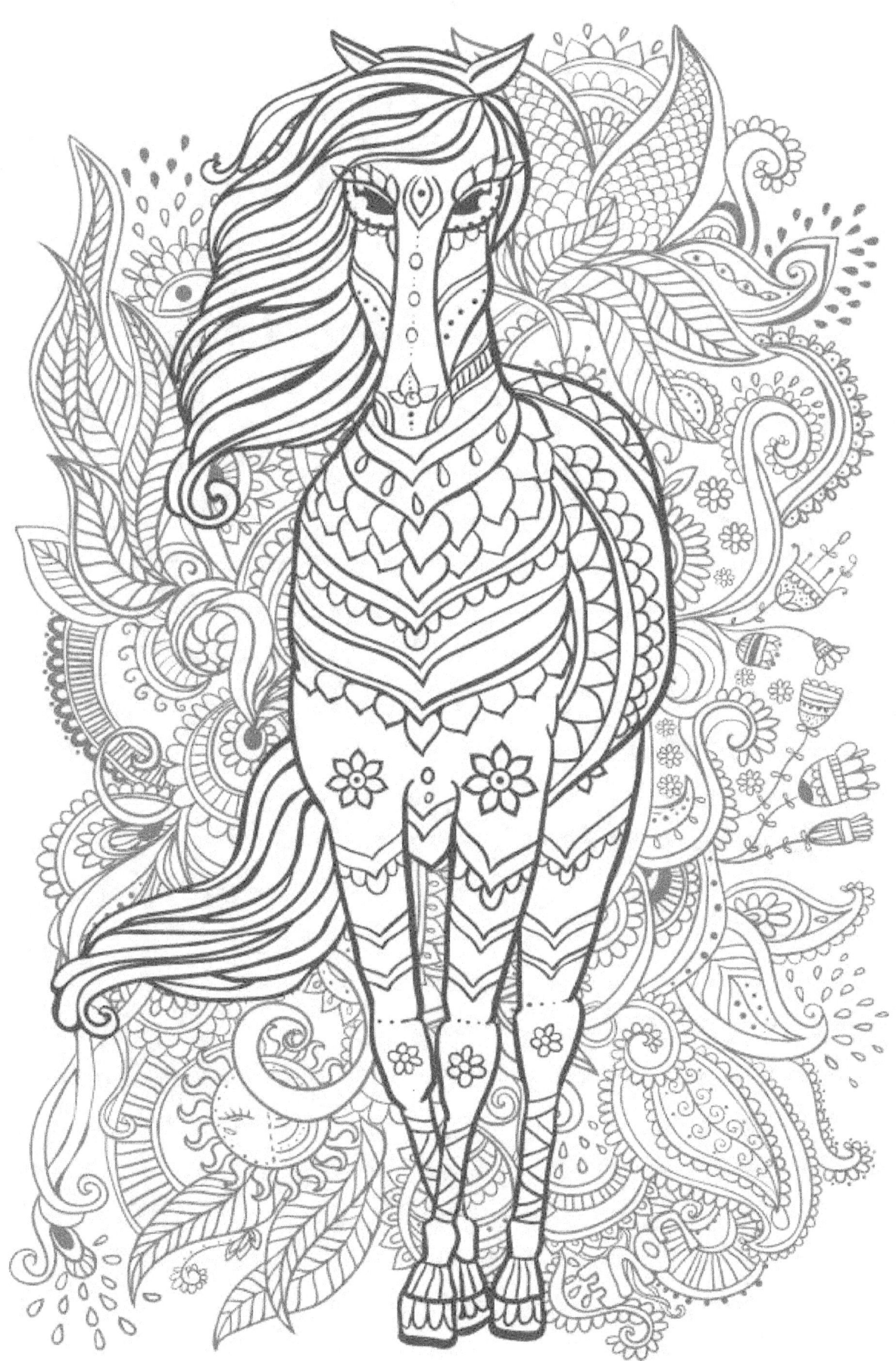

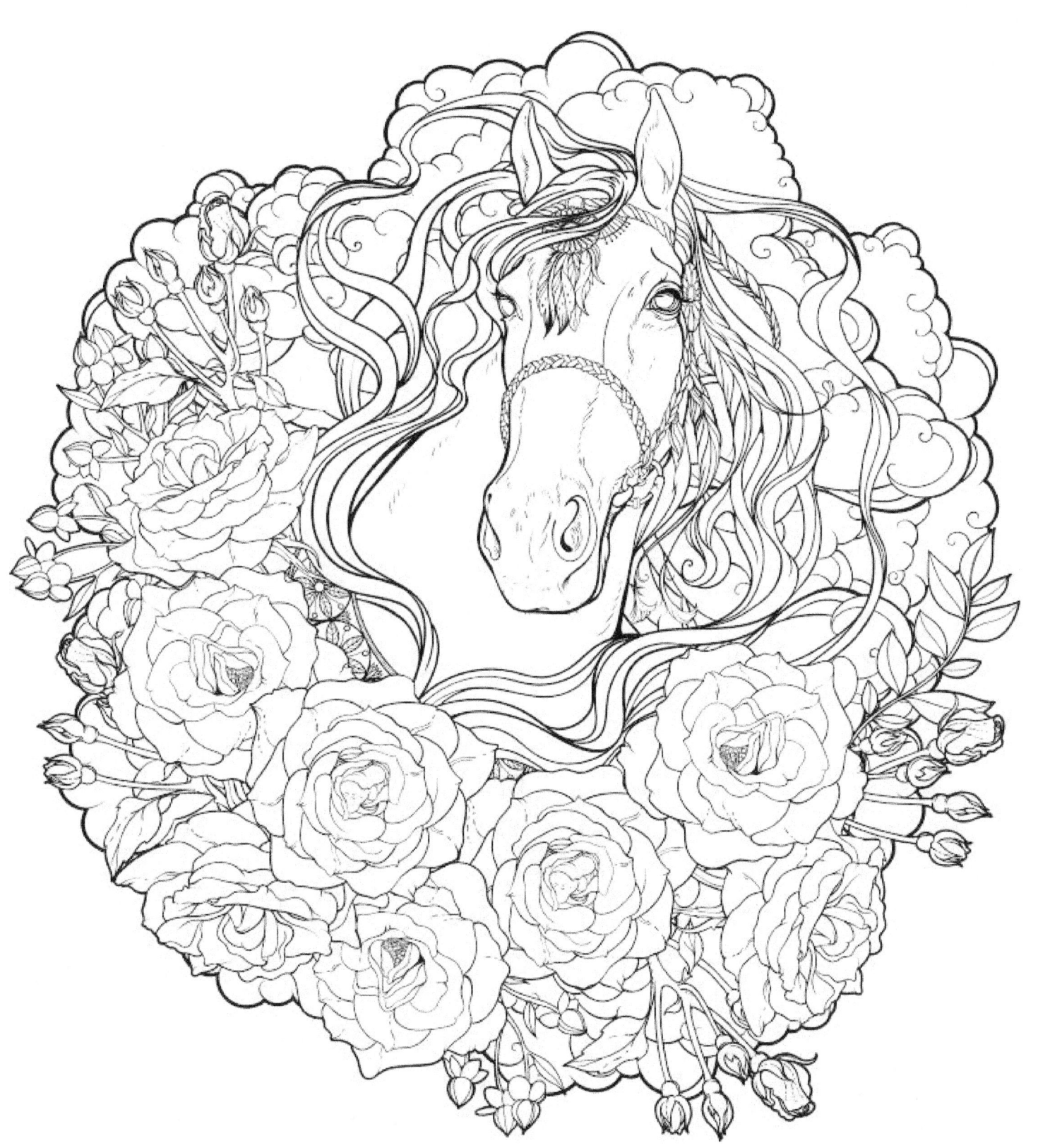

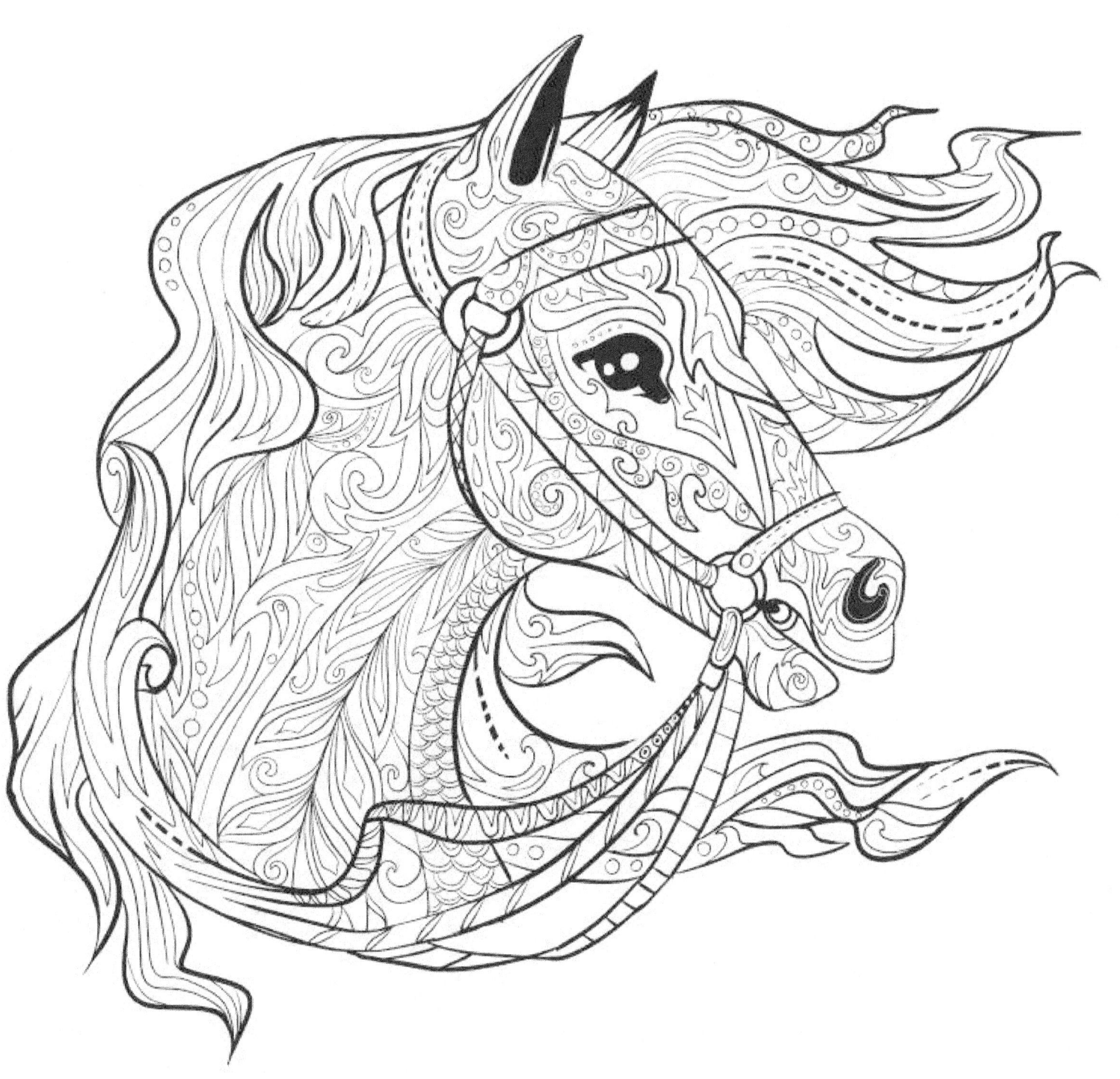

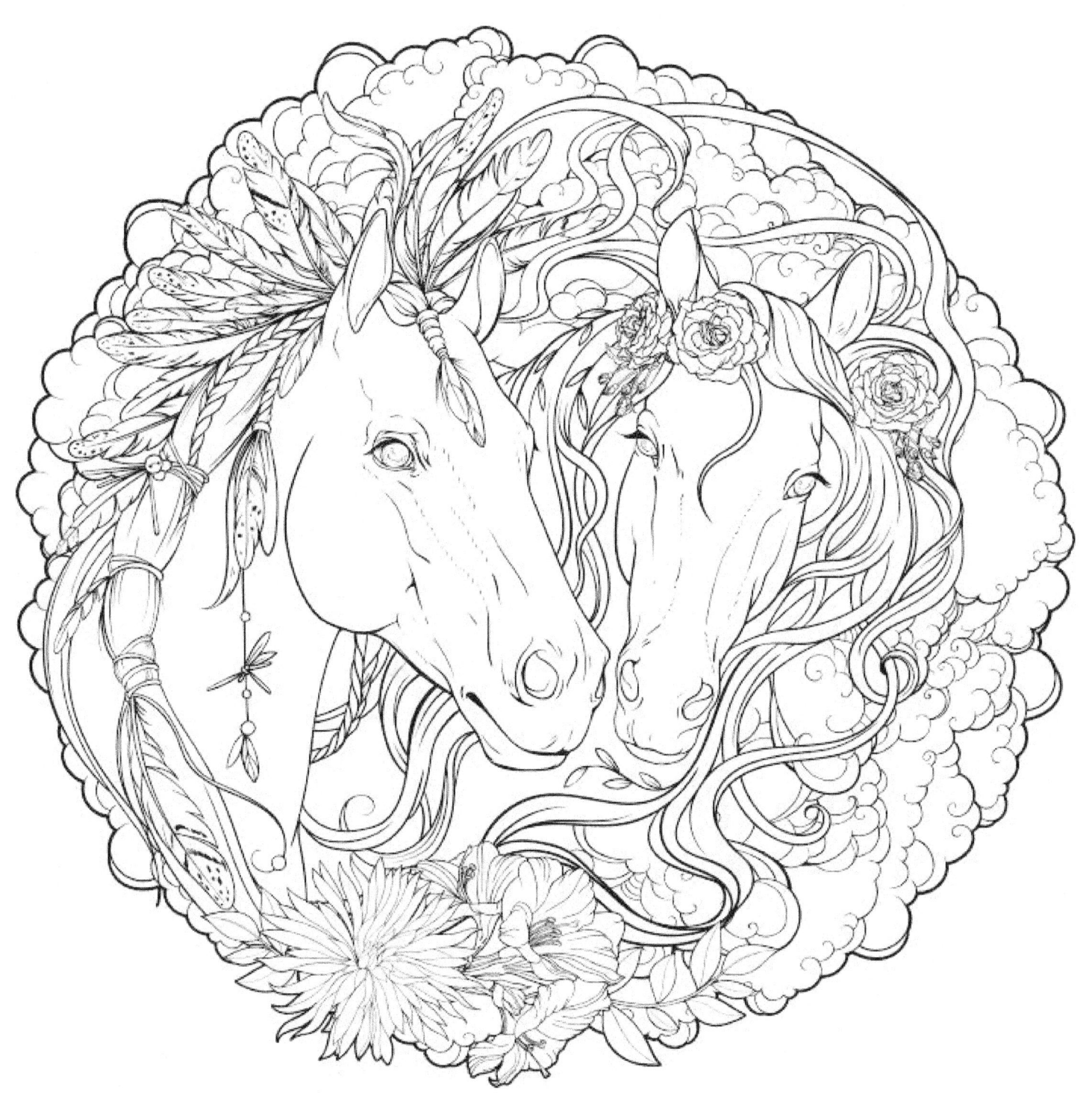

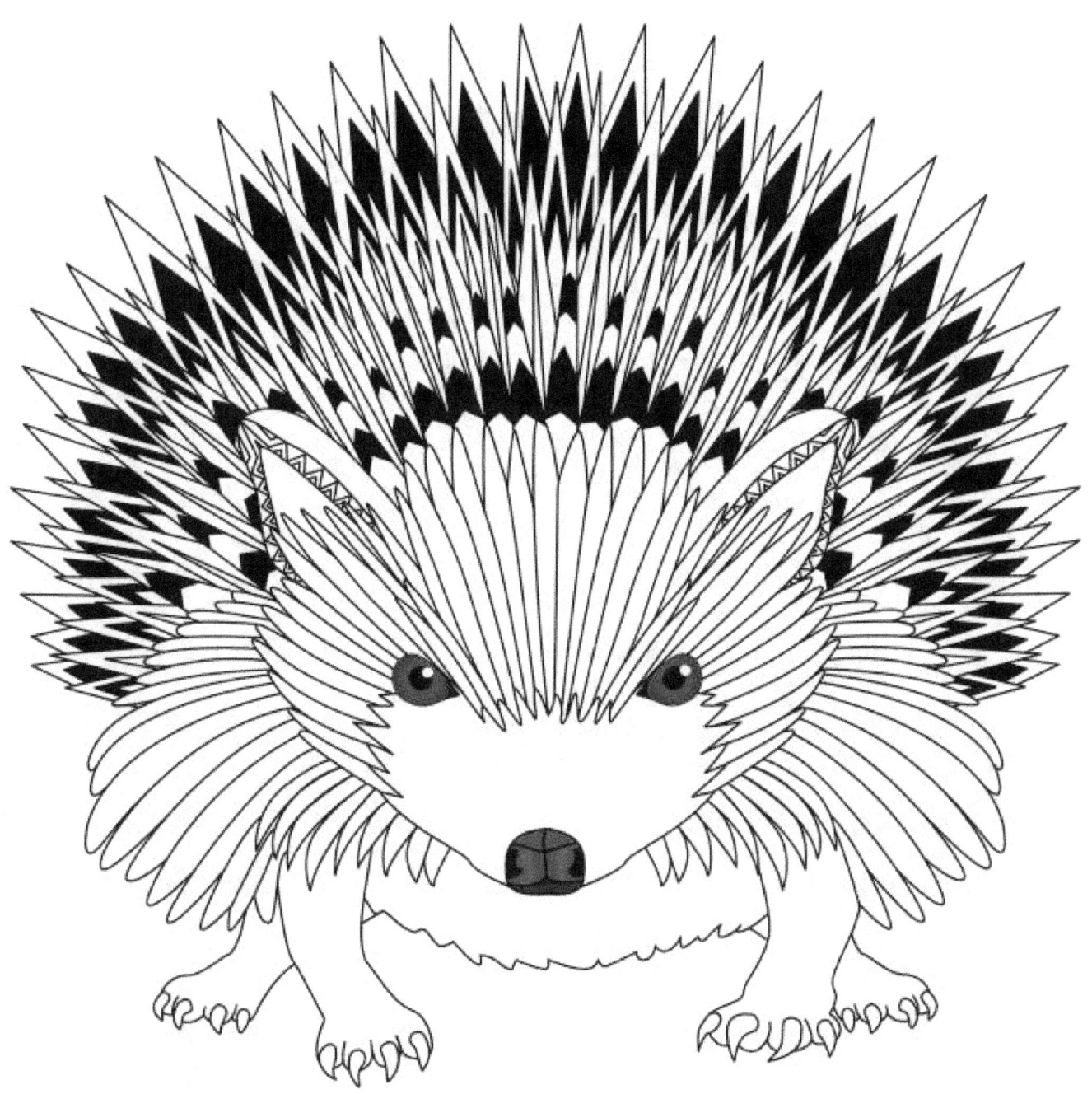

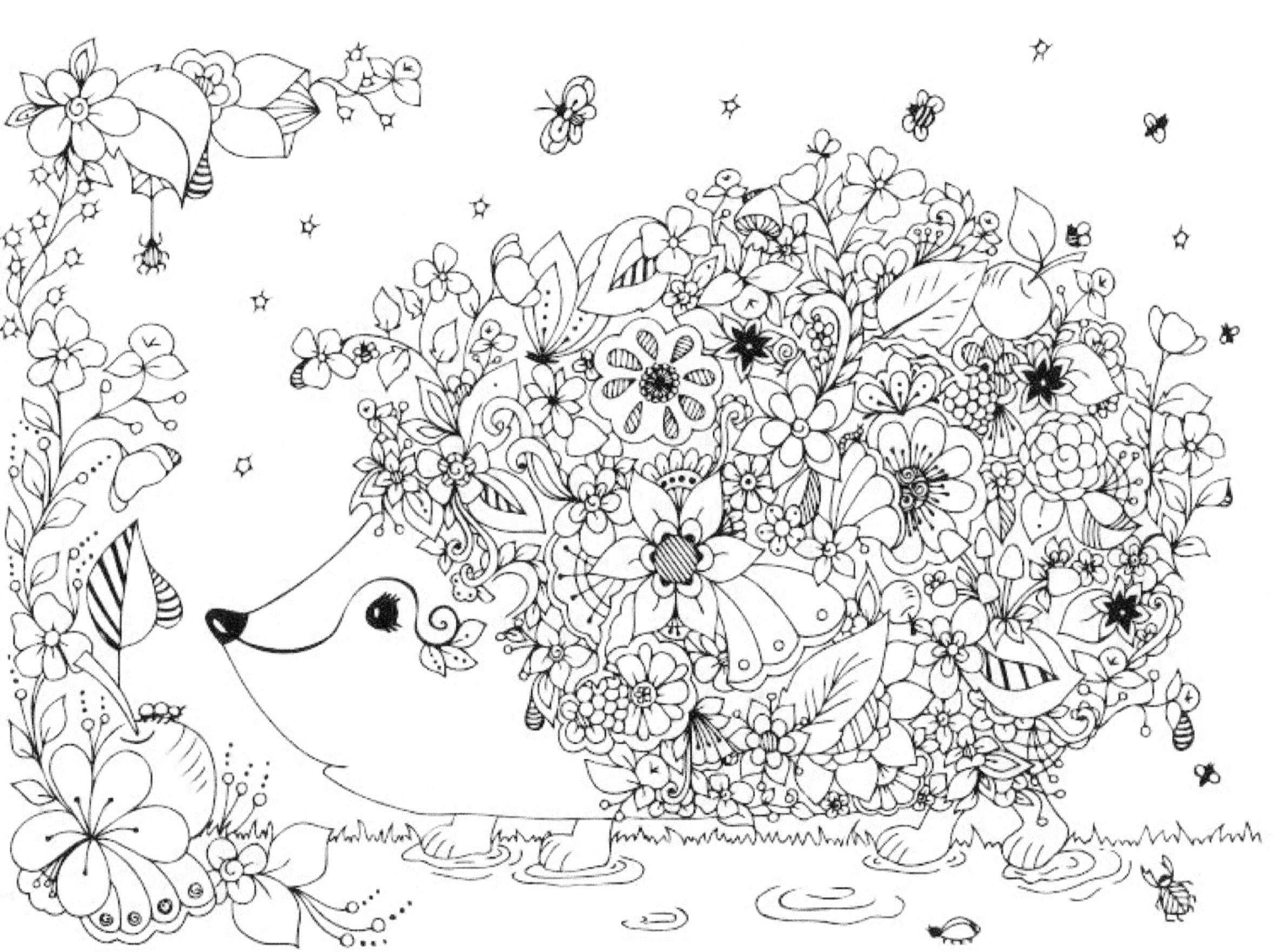

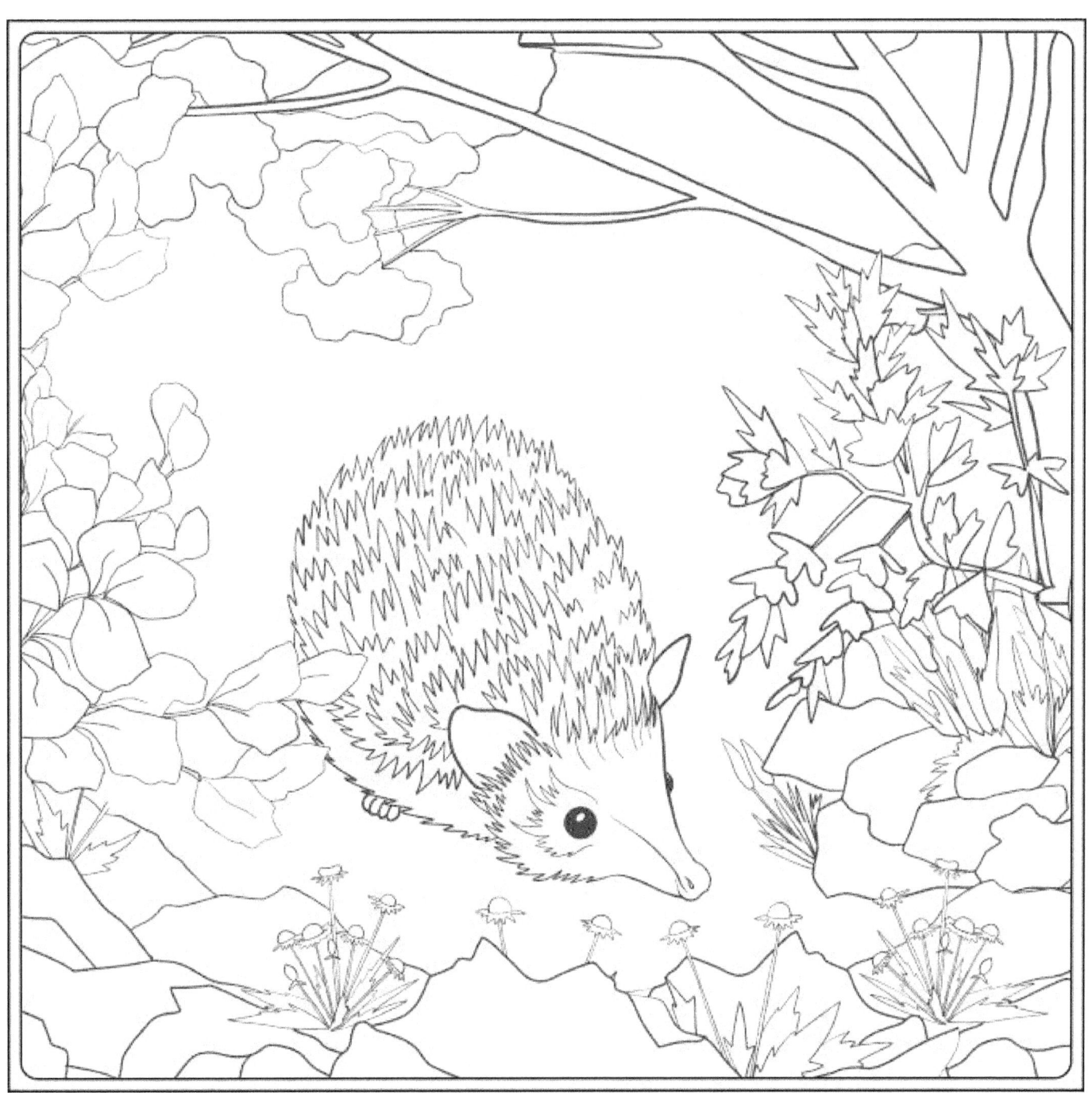

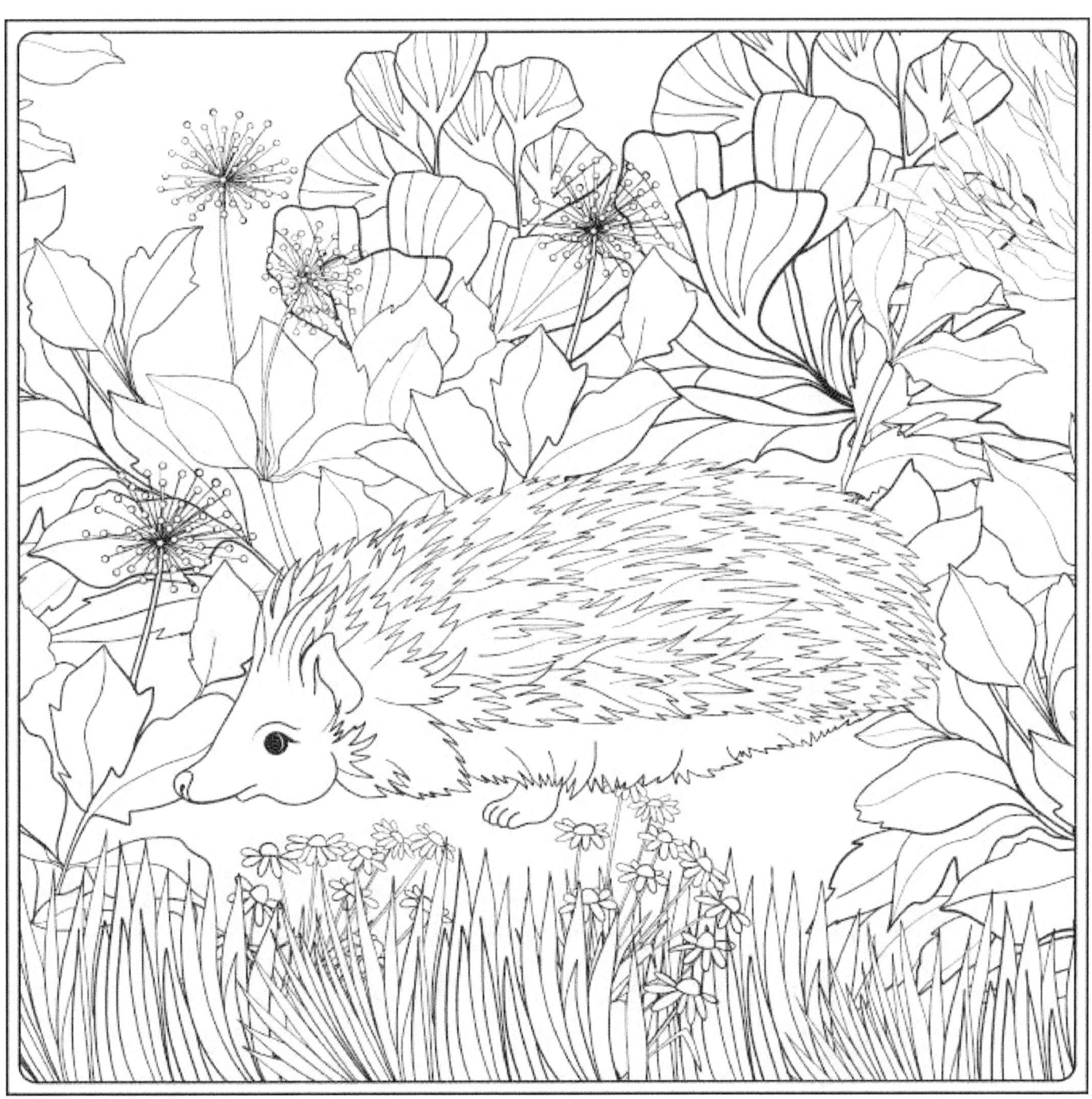

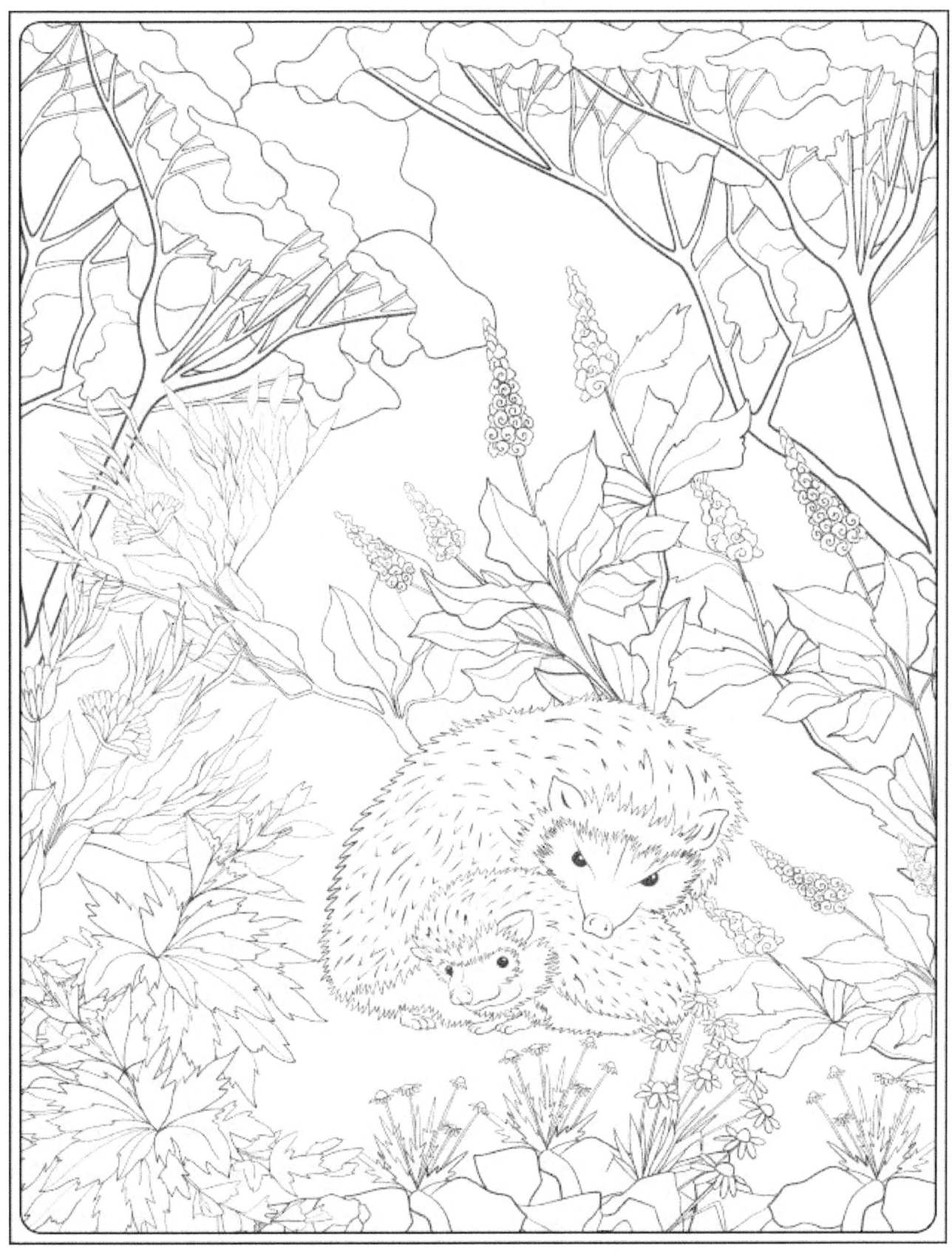

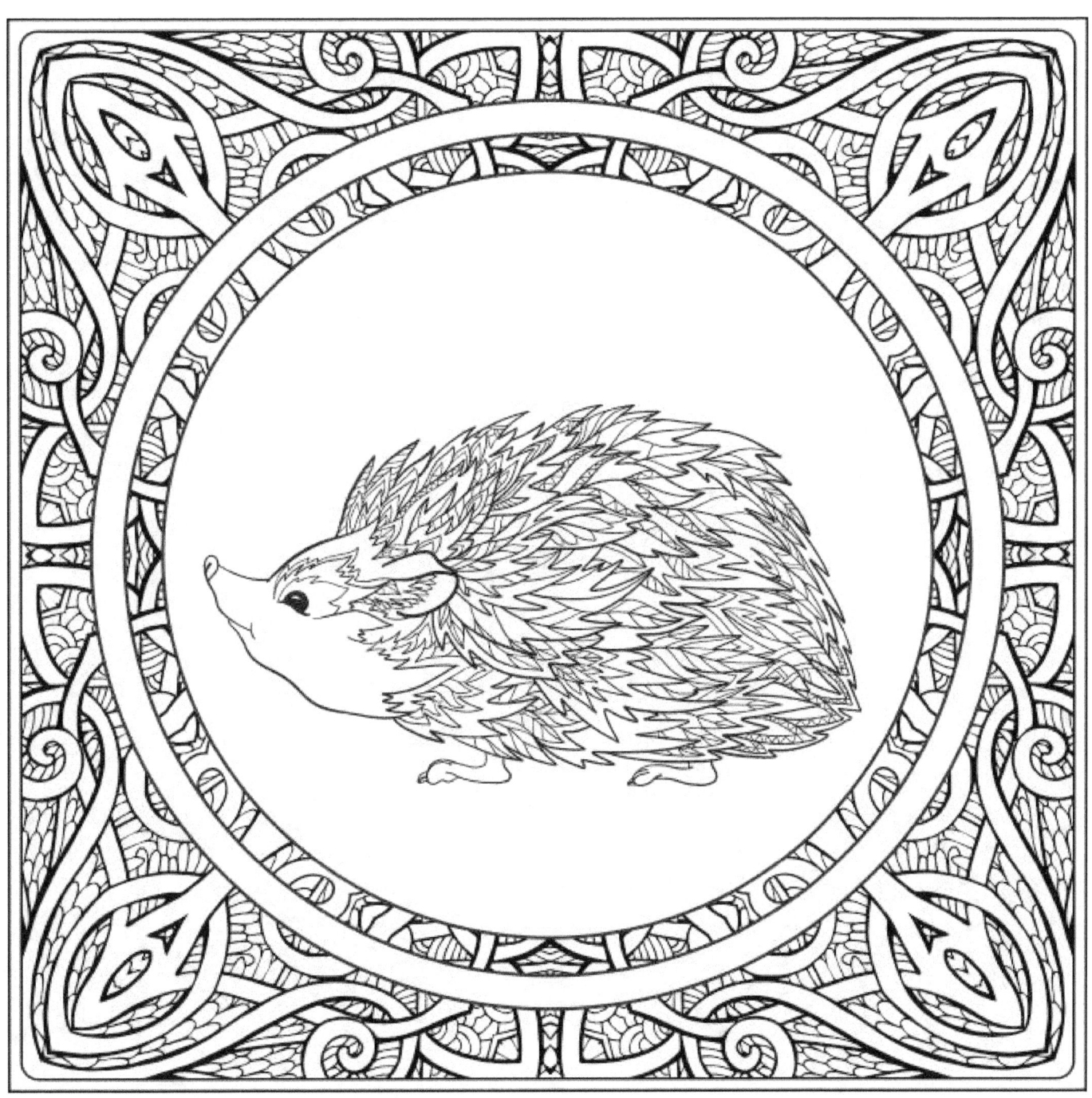

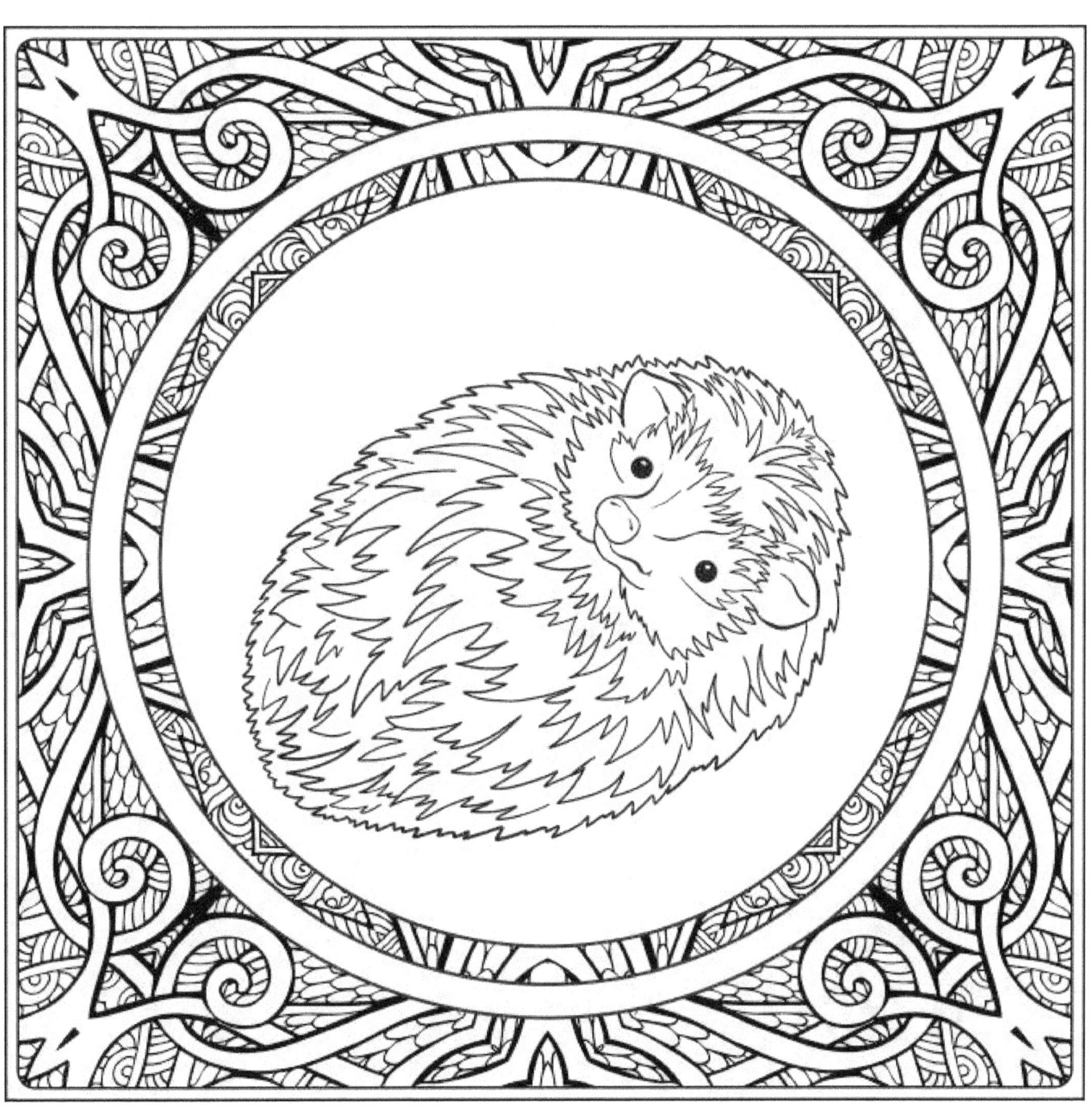

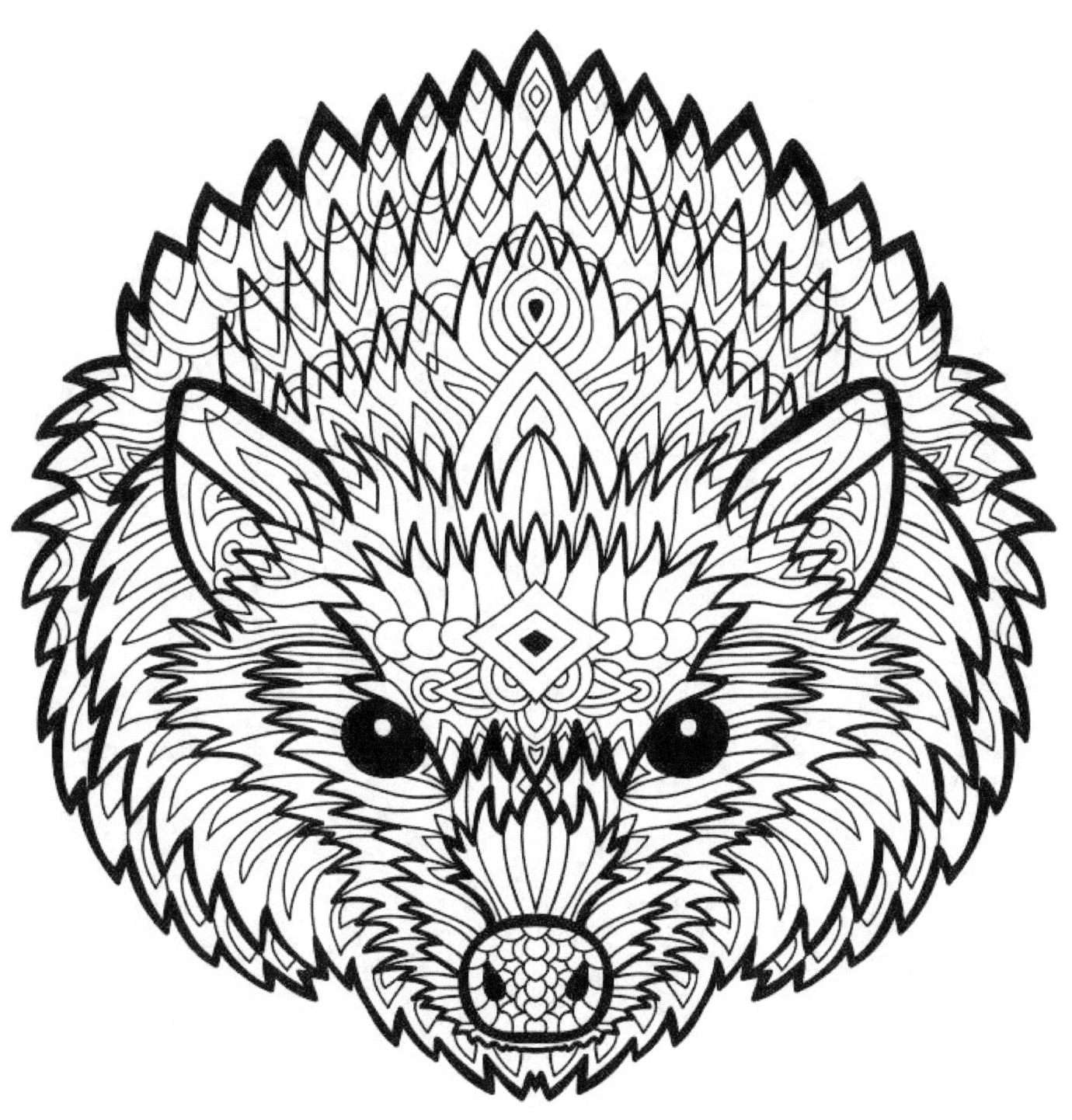

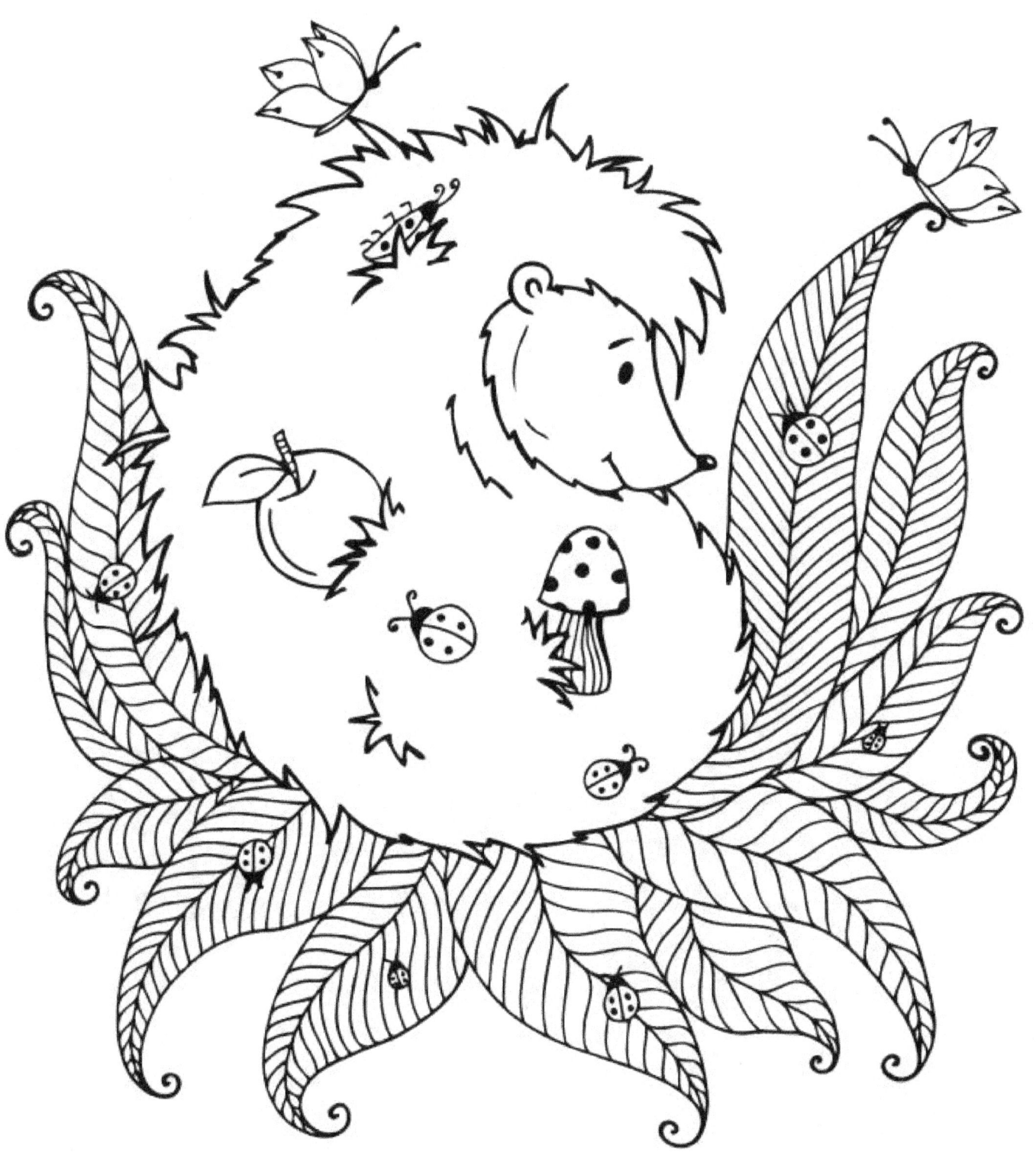

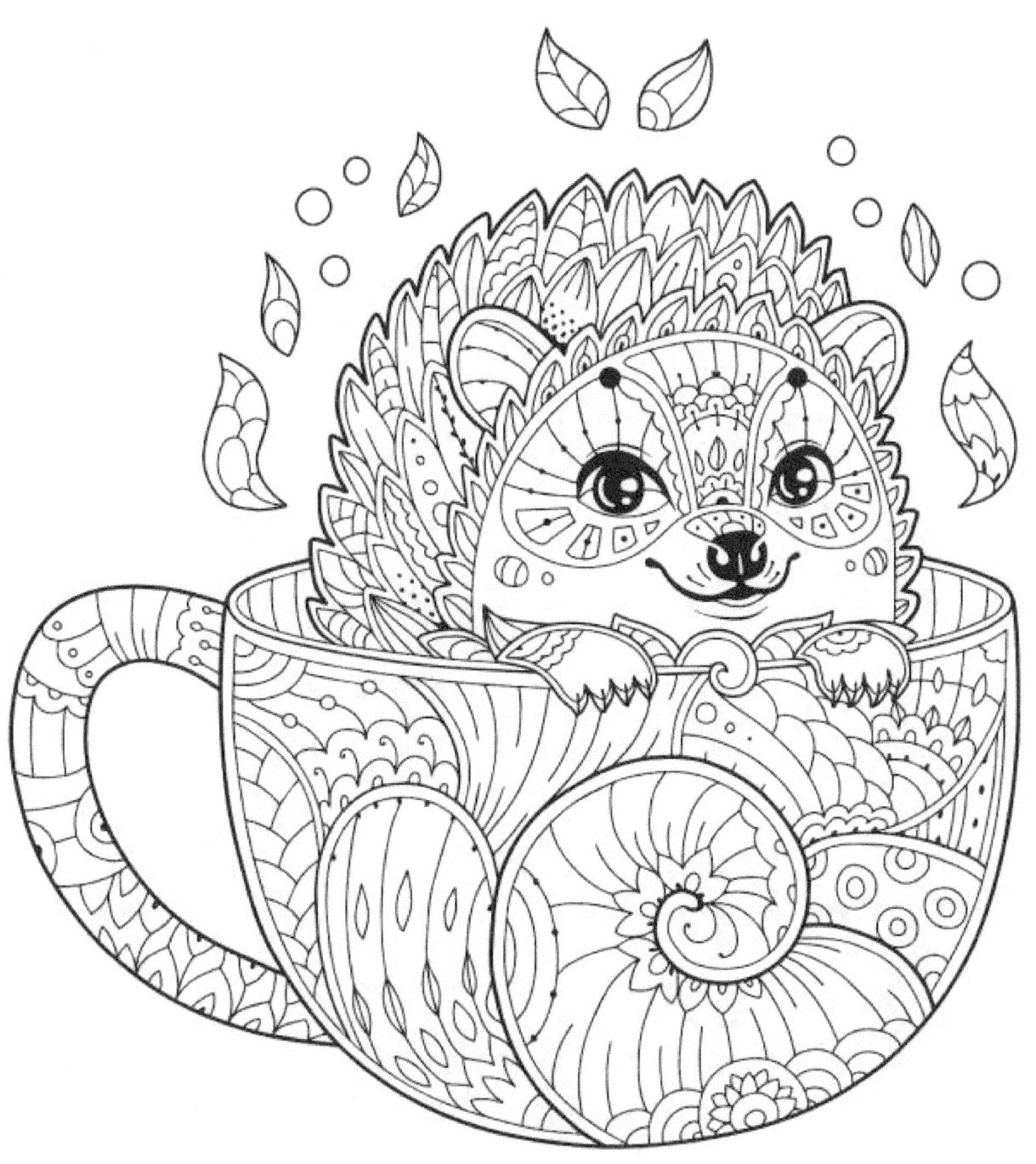

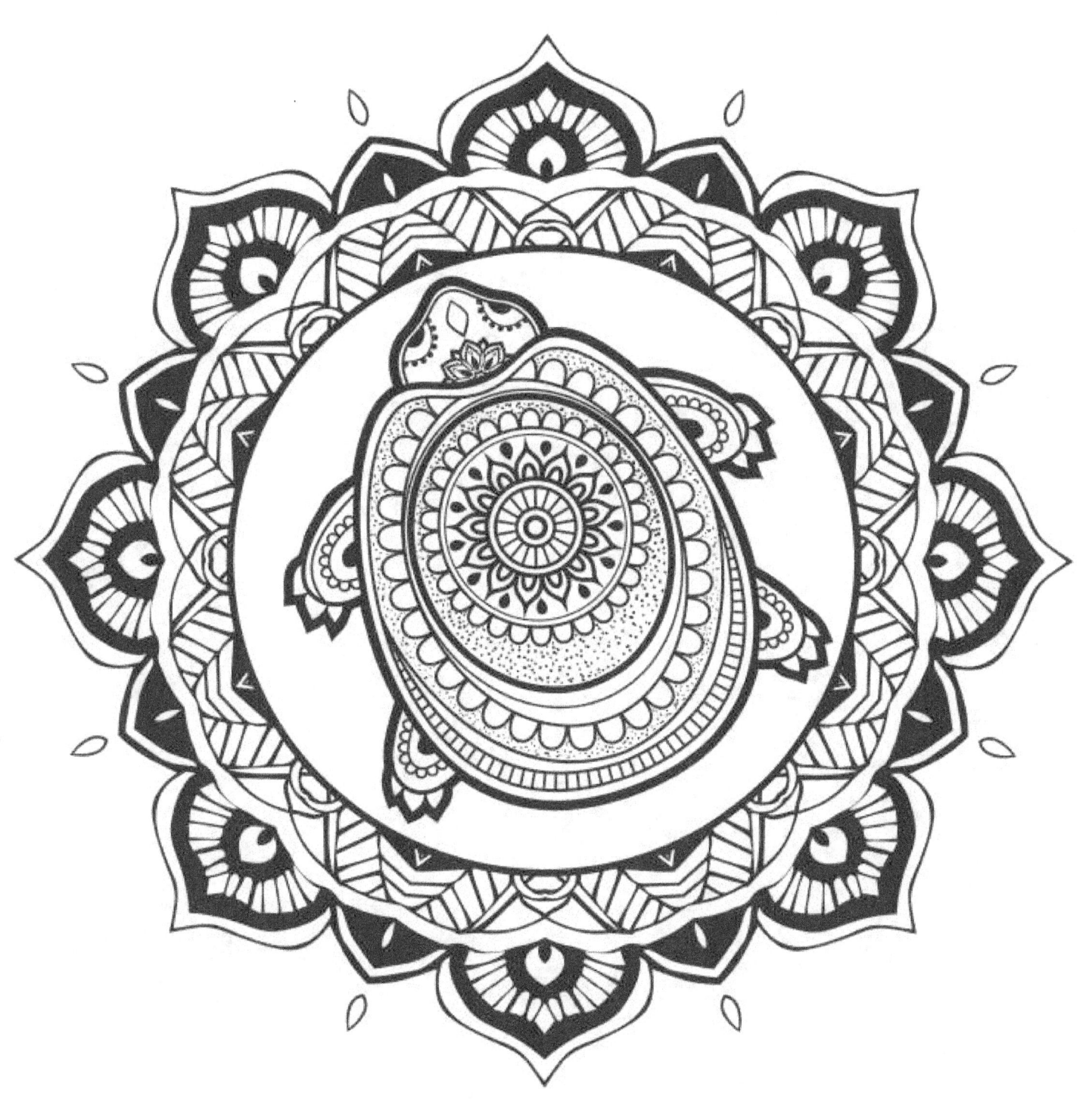

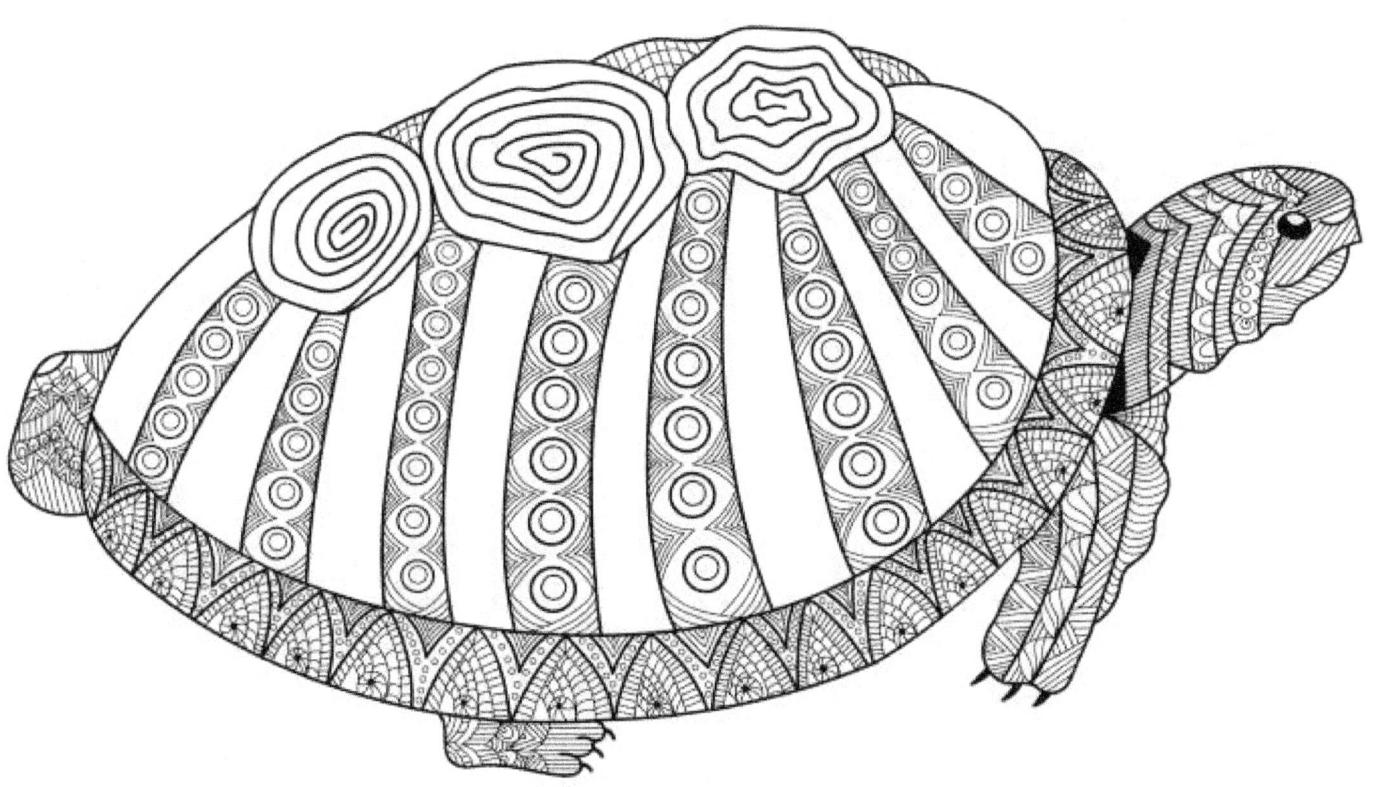

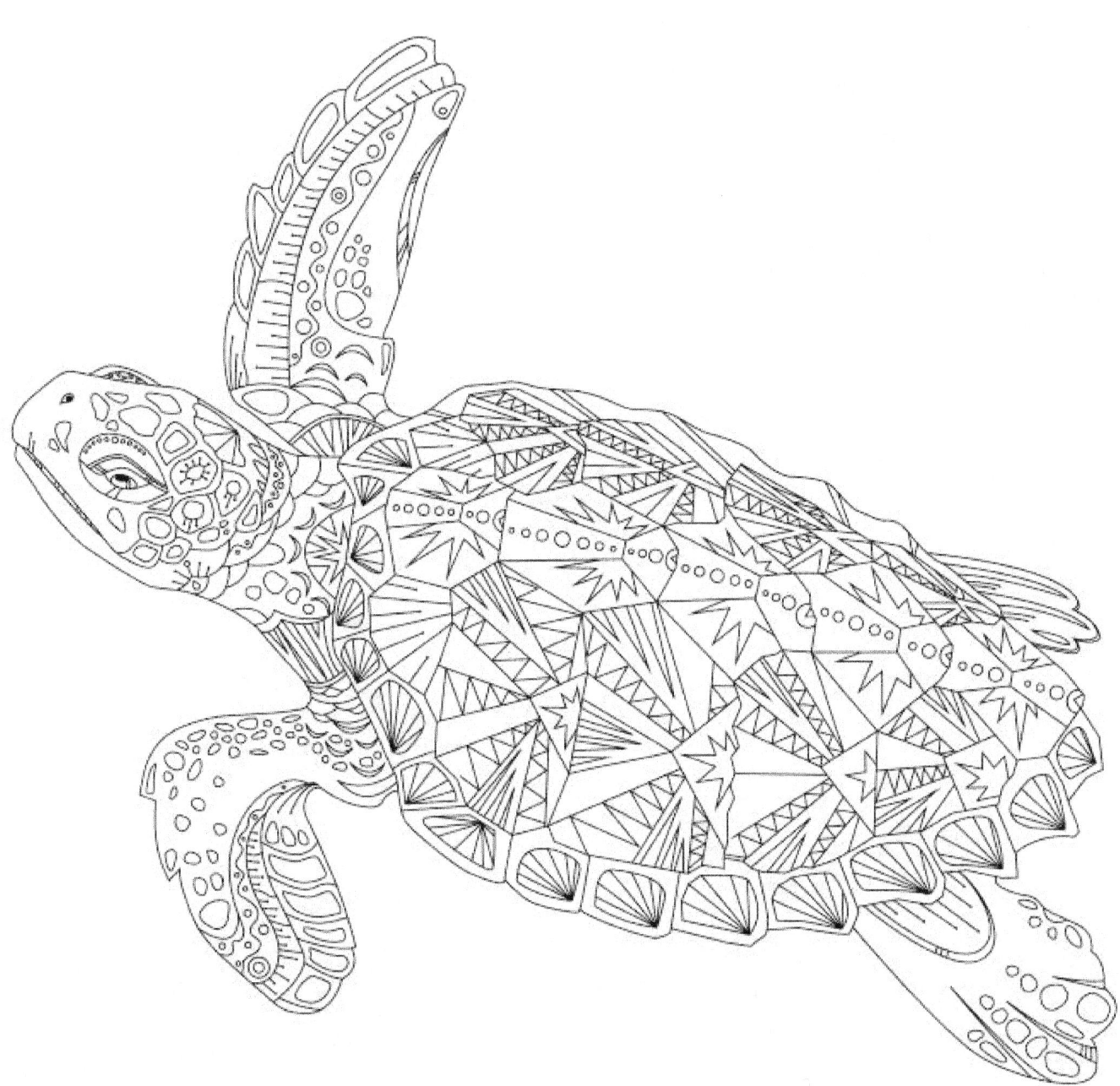

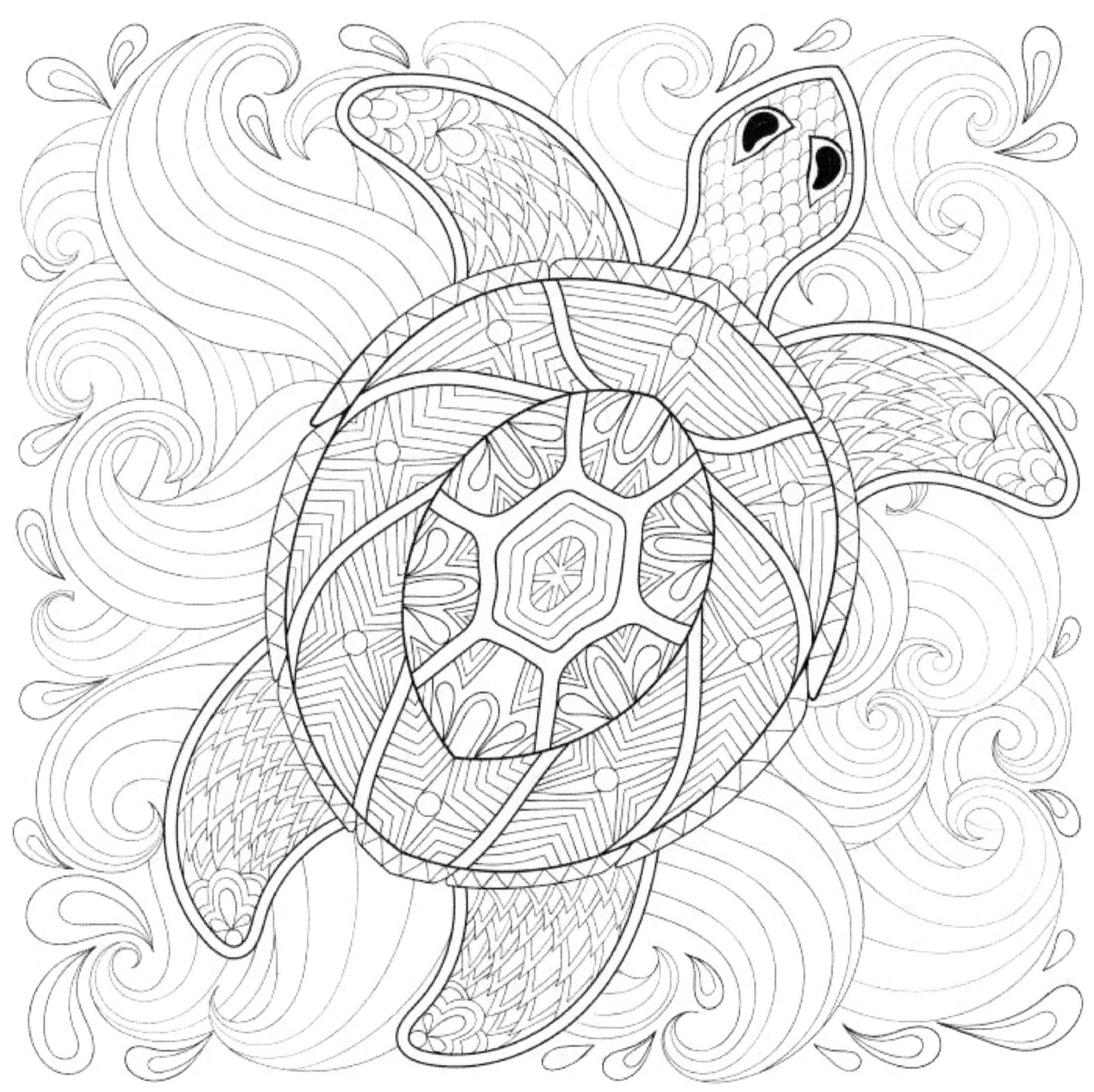

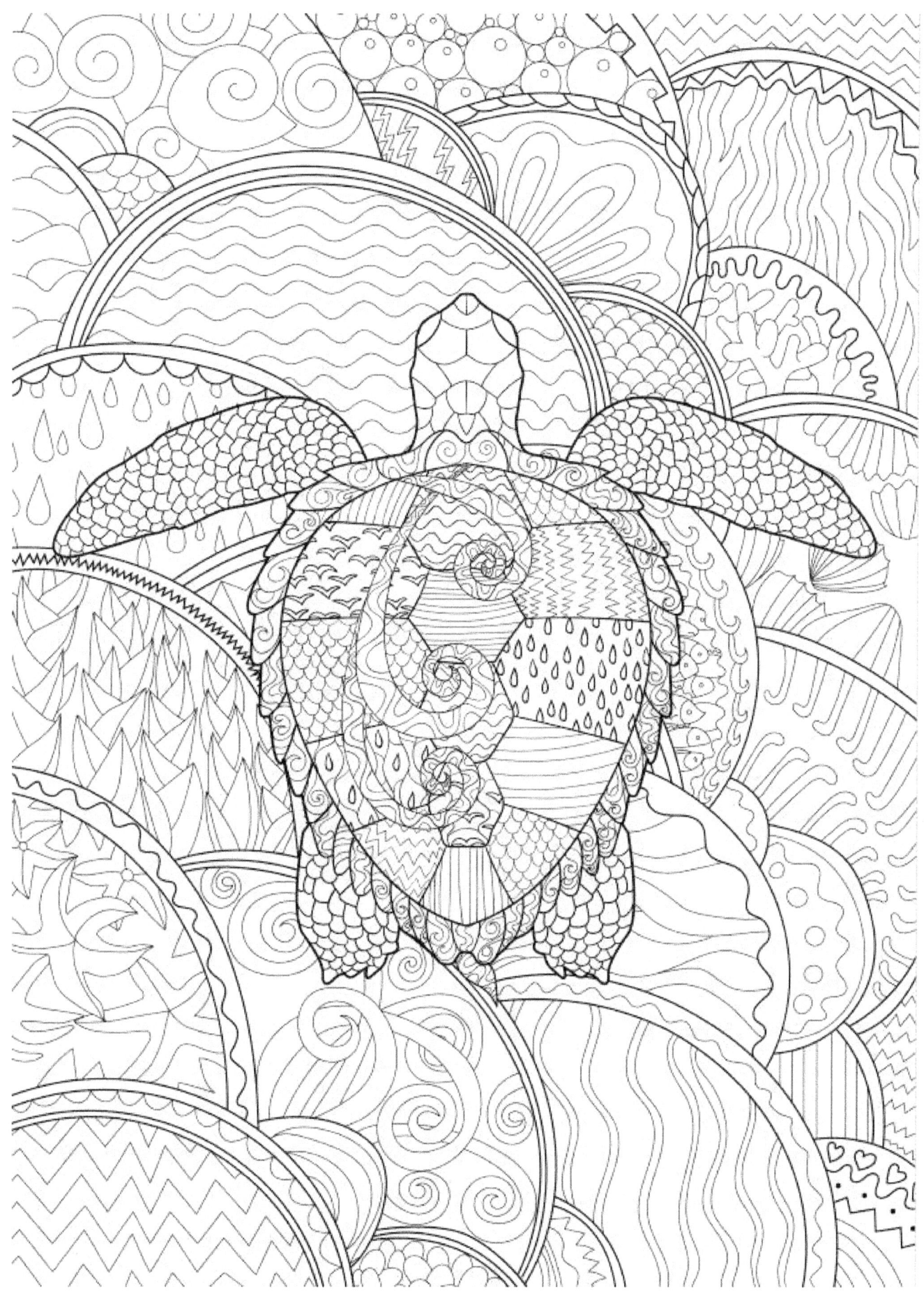

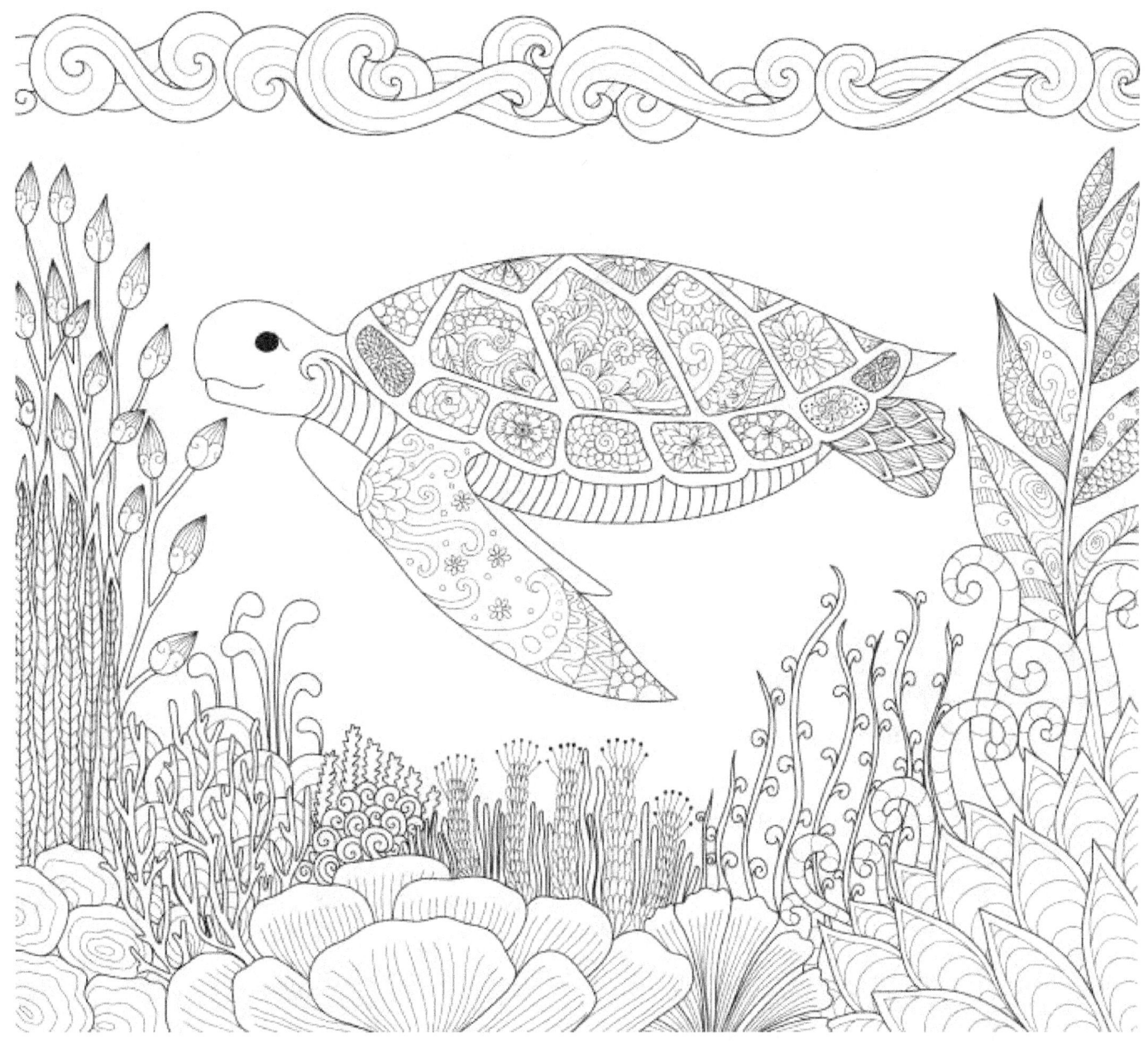

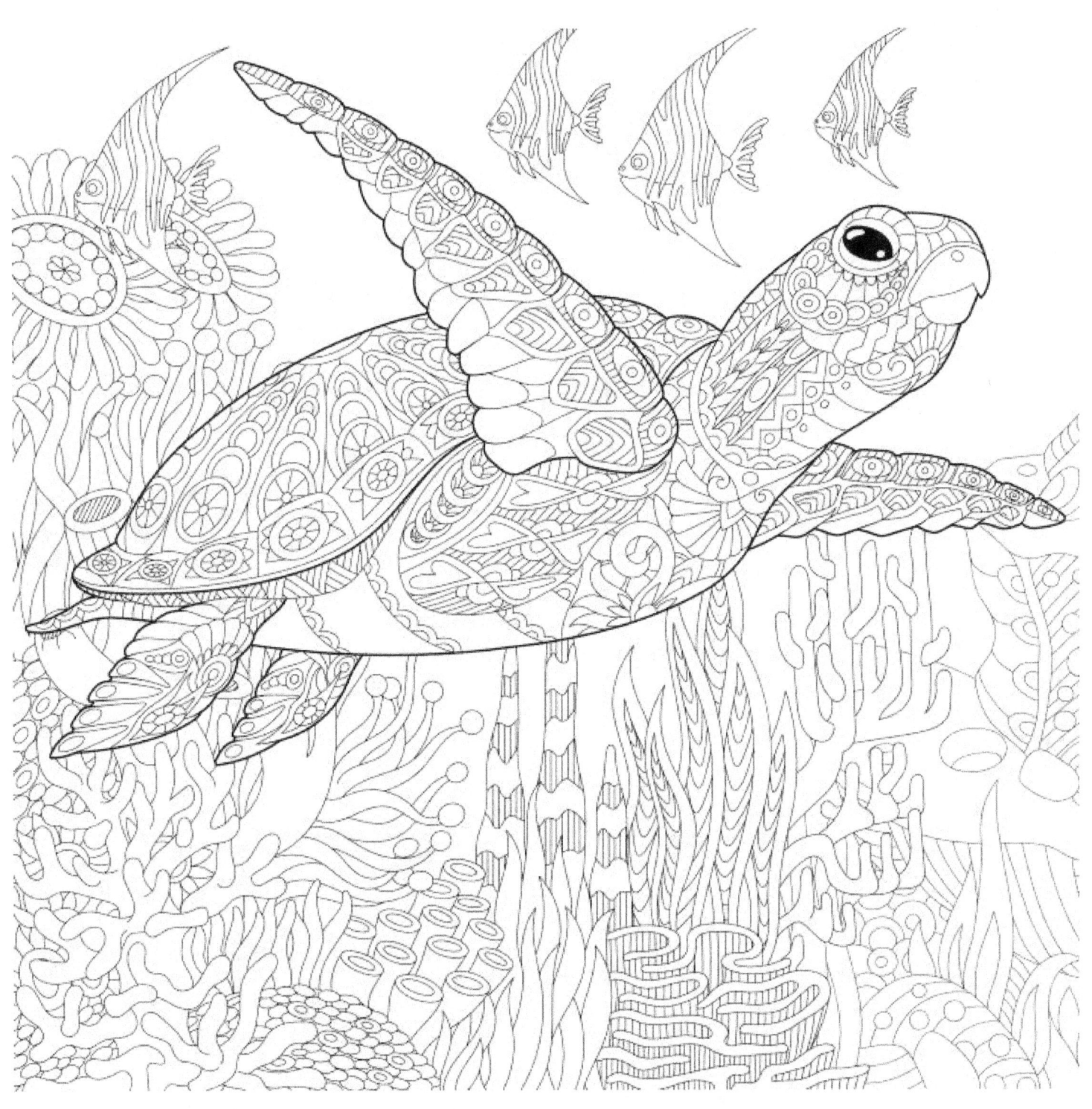

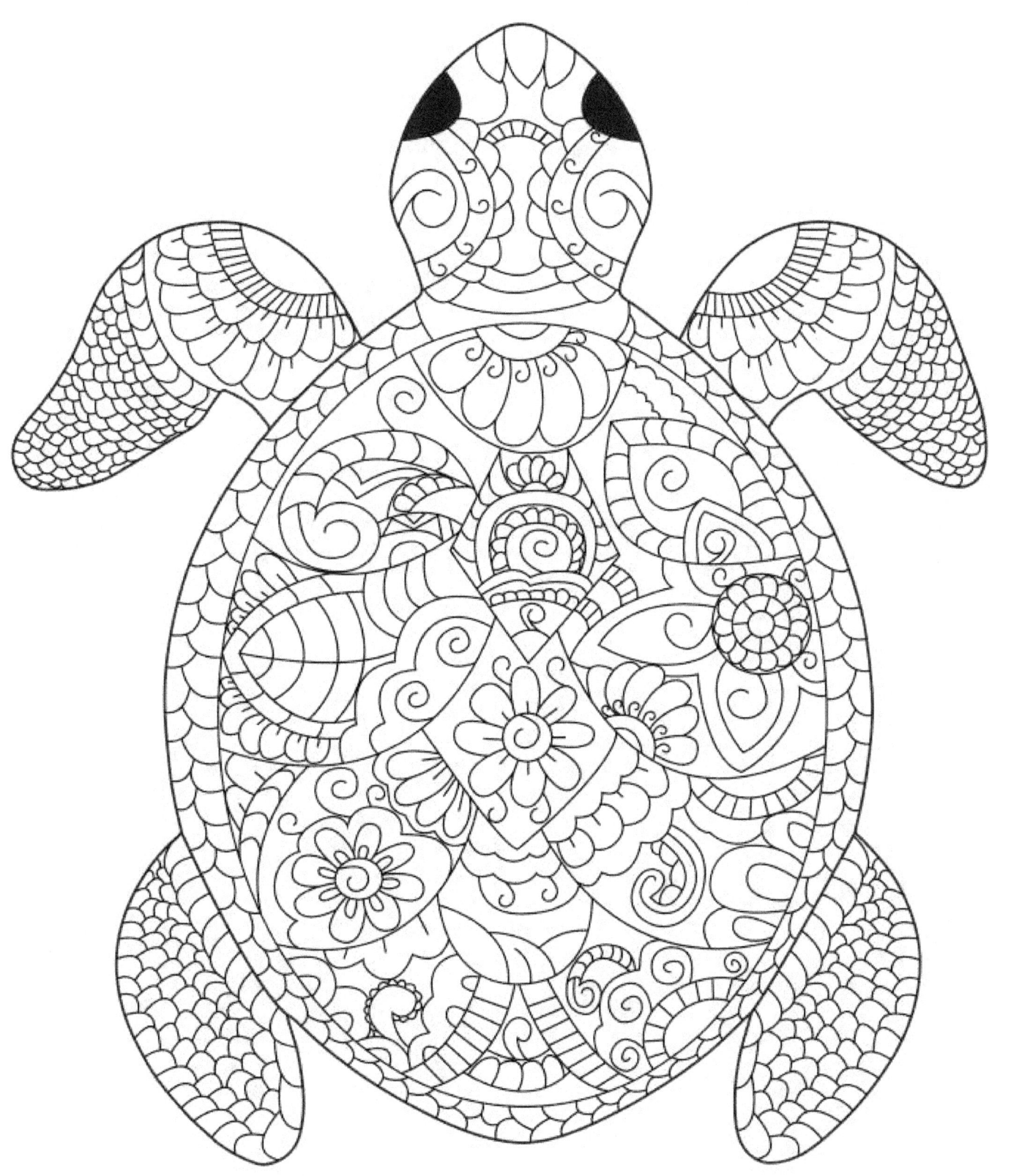

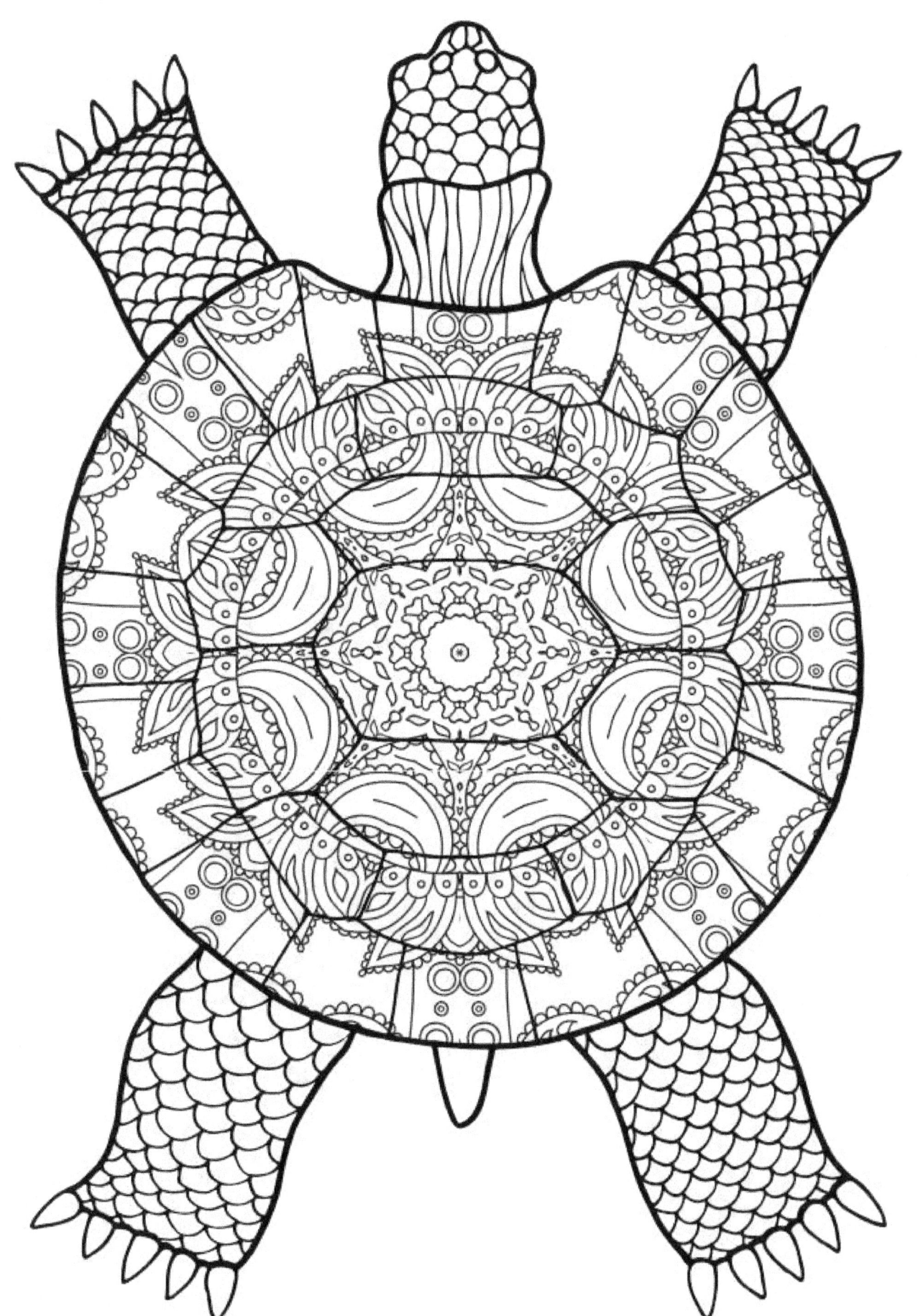

www.ingramcontent.com/pod-product-compliance
Lightning Source LLC
Chambersburg PA
CBHW081113180526
45170CB00008B/2833

* 9 7 8 1 5 4 6 7 6 2 4 0 9 *